Leave Me Alone with the Recipes

Edited by **SARAH RICH** and
with **MARIA POPOVA** and

LEAVE ME ALONE

WENDY MacNAUGHTON
DEBBIE MILLMAN

WITH THE RECIPES

THE LIFE,

ART, and

COOKBOOK

of *CIPE*

PINELES

BLOOMSBURY

New York London Oxford New Delhi Sydney

Bloomsbury USA
An imprint of Bloomsbury Publishing Plc

1385 Broadway   50 Bedford Square
New York   London
NY 10018   WC1B 3DP
USA   UK

www.bloomsbury.com

BLOOMSBURY and the Diana logo are trademarks of Bloomsbury Publishing Plc

First published 2017
© The Estate of Cipe Pineles, Sarah Rich, Wendy MacNaughton, Debbie Millman,
Maria Popova, Maira Kalman, Steven Heller, Paula Scher, Mimi Sheraton, 2017

Images on the following pages courtesy of Cary Graphic Arts Collection,
Rochester Institute of Technology. Used by permission of the Cipe Pineles Estate: i, 3, 7, 16, 20, 27,
89, 90, 97, 101, 103, 107, 108, 110, 113, 114, 115, 116, 118, 119, 120, 129

ISBN: HB: 978-1-63286-713-1
ePub: 978-1-63286-715-5

LIBRARY OF CONGRESS CATALOGING-IN-PUBLICATION DATA
Names: Rich, Sarah C., editor. | MacNaughton, Wendy, editor. | Millman,
Debbie, editor. | Popova, Maria, editor. | Pineles, Cipe, 1908–1991. Leave
me alone with the recipes.
Title: Leave me alone with the recipes : the life, art, and cookbook of Cipe
Pineles / edited by Sarah Rich with Wendy MacNaughton, Debbie Millman, and Maria Popova.
Description: New York : Bloomsbury USA, an imprint of Bloomsbury Publishing
Plc, 2017. | Collection of essays about Pineles along with her hand
illustrated previously unpublished cookbook entitled Leave me alone with
the recipes. | Includes bibliographical references and index.
Identifiers: LCCN 2016059366| ISBN 978-1-63286-713-1 (hardcover) |
ISBN 978-1-63286-715-5 (ePub)
Subjects: LCSH: Cooking—Europe, Eastern. | Jewish cooking. | Pineles, Cipe,
1908–1991. | Graphic artists—United States—Biography. | LCGFT: Cookbooks.
Classification: LCC TX723.5.A1 L36 2017 | DDC 641.594—dc23
LC record available at https://lccn.loc.gov/2016059366

2 4 6 8 10 9 7 5 3

Designed by de Vicq Design
Printed in China by RR Donnelley Asia Printing Solutions Limited

To find out more about our authors and books visit www.bloomsbury.com.
Here you will find extracts, author interviews, details of forthcoming events
and the option to sign up for our newsletters.

Bloomsbury books may be purchased for business or promotional use.
For information on bulk purchases please contact
Macmillan Corporate and Premium Sales Department at
specialmarkets@macmillan.com.

For Charlotte Sheedy

CONTENTS

This story begins in a massive exhibition hall on a chilly February day in San Francisco. On a whim, I decided to spend a Saturday morning with my friend the illustrator Wendy MacNaughton, browsing the aisles of the California International Antiquarian Book Fair—the kind of activity that complements fog.

If you were to paint a picture of this scene, the palette would be a muted one—book jackets gone from red to rusty brown, emerald to muted gray. Bold, bright colors aren't what one expects from a bunch of books whose common theme is old age. And yet. The climactic moment of our visit to the fair could only be captured in the most brilliant hues, for the work we found that morning felt as new and bright as if the paint had been laid down yesterday. We were stopped in our tracks by a woman we'd never heard of and would never be lucky enough to meet, but would spend the next three years getting to know.

My husband and I were late coming over from Oakland, and as we drove across the bridge, I received a text from Wendy. She had found something mind-blowing that I had to see right away. She'd spotted a sketchbook propped open in a glass case, displaying a painting of a bowl of soup with some lettering around it. The bowl was a bright mint green, scalloped with a darker pine to form the shape. The soup within was a brilliant, hot fuchsia. The image popped off the page. This solid block of color was contrasted with a title rendered in perfect typeface, but completely hand-painted: "Borscht."

INTRODUCTION: DISCOVERING CIPE SARAH RICH

And below that was a long hand-written recipe lettered in script so fine it could have been made with a feather quill. The composition was charming; loose, but perfect. The whole piece was spectacular.

Wendy had asked the bookseller if she could take a closer look. Once it was out from behind the glass, it was clear this wasn't a reproduction but an original. The date on the title page was 1945. The soup bowl was painted with gouache in the manner one is taught in the most rigorous courses in art school—an agonizing process of mixing gouache paint and water to a precise consistency so that the paint lays even and smooth on the page, almost powder-coating the paper into a chalky, velvet finish. And the lettering, up close, revealed all the beautiful imperfections of hand-painted type. The artist nearly perfectly mimicked a typeface she must have known very well, but the quirks of the human hand holding the pen are what made it so unique and special.

When we reached her, Wendy was nearly manic with the thrill of the discovery. She'd learned from the bookseller that indeed, the artist mimicked typeface like a pro because she was one; she had been an art director at Condé Nast beginning in the 1930s and had taught at Parsons School of Design for decades.

As Wendy raved about the incredible technique, I began turning the pristine pages, thrilled by the recipes themselves. This was my family's food—the Old World, Eastern European Jewish cuisine that my grandmother and great-grandmother had made again and again in their kitchens—brought to life through the hand of this remarkable artist. Having spent years trying to merge my design writing with my love of food and cooking, I felt like I was staring at the heart of my personal Venn diagram. And I was stirred by the idea that this humble, traditional food could be celebrated so boldly through art. There was nothing boring about Cipe's borscht.

Both Wendy and I felt like we had seen this work somewhere before. It was familiar but fresh. The style was both nostalgic and contemporary. It looked like the art of so many of our favorite current illustrators. It also looked a great deal like Wendy's own work. To her, it felt as if she'd modeled her style after this person's art without ever knowing she existed.

We leafed through dozens of pages, each a recipe for a dish profiled in paint and words—sprays of parsley, piles of beans, and collections of metal cookware and wooden utensils. There was brisket and stuffed cabbage rolls, kasha and kugel. In the back of the book were unfinished illustrations of gefilte fish and hamantaschen—the images complete but lettering missing—yet there was no mistaking what they were.

The artist's name was Cipe Pineles. We stood googling her on our phones, combing through the scant information that turned up. She'd emigrated from Europe in 1915 at the age of eight and worked at Condé Nast as their first female art director and the designer behind numerous popular magazines, including *Mademoiselle*, *Glamour*, *Vanity Fair*, and *Vogue*. Andy Warhol once called her his favorite art director. Ben Shahn was a regular among her pool of editorial illustrators. To the two of us—one an artist and the other a magazine editor—her name should perhaps have been familiar. Yet it wasn't. Why had we never heard of Cipe Pineles?

She'd been married to two graphic designers who enjoyed fame and recognition during their lifetimes, yet her own influence was relatively unsung. And these paintings, the ones we encountered three thousand miles away from Pineles's home and two decades after her death, had never been published or even seen beyond her immediate family.

We were captivated. We wanted to learn more about this woman and we wanted her name and work to be more widely known, since her influence had so clearly made its way down to the current generation of artists. We dialed our friends in New York, Maria Popova and Debbie Millman, breathlessly sharing our discovery and asking if they'd want to join us in shining a brighter light on this amazing woman. Together, the four of us purchased her sketchbook. We stored it carefully wrapped in a fireproof safe and set out to find a publisher.

Photographic portrait of Cipe Pineles by Trude Fleischmann

3

The road from then to now was paved with serendipity. Our literary agent, Charlotte Sheedy, turned out to have been friends with Cipe in New York. She'd been to her storied dinner parties and they shared many friends. Through Charlotte, we located Joel Corcos Levy, a close family friend of Cipe's. Joel introduced us to Carol Burtin Fripp, whom Cipe had adopted after marrying Will Burtin, Carol's father, in 1961.

We flew to Toronto during an unseasonably cold late May to meet Carol and ask her blessing to pursue this project. Carol had moved into Cipe's house in Stony Point, New York, when she was eighteen years old, soon after her father became Cipe's second husband. She now lives in Canada with her husband, Robert, in a home lined from floor to ceiling with art and books by Cipe and her creative collaborators. We sat with Carol, Robert, and Cipe's grandson, Will, on the classic mid-century furniture handed down from Carol's father. We showed them the original paintings that had come into our possession, and Carol recalled seeing some of them decades earlier at Cipe's Stony Point house.

Even to the people most familiar with Cipe and her work, the charm and freshness of these paintings was remarkable. Stories poured forth from Carol, Robert, and Will—memories of parties and family dinners and quiet weekends together. We toured the Fripp house and Will showed us cards his grandmother Cipe had sent him for his childhood birthdays, which she decorated with elaborate illustration and hand-hewn typography. In the front hall hung a padded envelope addressed to Carol and Robert in perfect calligraphy, covered in assorted stamps Cipe had collected; in the bathroom was a card she'd painted with the names of Carol's family members, bidding them farewell after a visit. Robert told stories of meeting Cipe when he and Carol were first dating.

If Cipe was known for something beyond her design prowess, we learned, it was her love of—and gift for—entertaining. She loved to throw dinner parties and did so often, assembling some of the most influential artists, writers, designers, and thinkers of her day around a table of food and drink.

Her mother's recipes, the ones that appear in her sketchbook, were not, for the most part, what she served at these parties. Cipe's cooking reflected the culinary trends of mid-century New York, with French and other international influences. Her archive contains recipe clippings from the *New York Times* Food section, the *Chicago Sun-Times*, and various magazines, for things such as cheese straws, sausage rolls, short ribs à la française, paella, cranberry whipped cream salad, quiche lorraine, and risotto à la suisse.

For many years, Cipe had cooking help from a housekeeper named Roslyn Rose ("Ros"). Carol said that before moving to Stony Point, "I'd never lived in a house which had a person doing the cooking and laundry. To me it was luxurious. There was that sense of plenty." Carol remembers Ros and Cipe working alongside each other in the kitchen, turning out eggplant parmesan and brown rice with beans. "After Ros retired, Cipe did the cooking," Carol remembers, "She specialized in pot roast and in the summertime we sometimes had whole meals that were nothing but the best, freshest corn on the cob and tomatoes and basil from the garden and some French bread."

It wasn't just the food to which Cipe dedicated her creative attention, but all the details surrounding the meal. The table would be beautifully set, each plate accompanied by a cloth napkin made from a Liberty print, sewn by Cipe herself. Each diner had a different pattern on his or her napkin, and visitors who were staying for more than one meal knew which place was theirs by the pattern they'd been given for the duration of their stay. The food Cipe served her guests wasn't fancy—she kept things simple—but it was always plentiful, and her taste was evident in each dish. "If there was dessert, it was some kind of babka or if it was ice cream, only vanilla," Carol remembers. "I wondered if she felt that way about white bread, if early on when she'd tasted white bread in France en route to the U.S. it was an eye-opening experience. We didn't have other flavors in the house. My father would take me to Dairy Queen and we'd have our hot fudge sundae."

The Jewish recipes, Carol said, weren't things Cipe made at home, but were eaten

4

with family on holidays. "We would go, usually not on the actual day—and for us Yom Kippur was not a day of fasting, it was a day of feasting—we'd go to Regine's house [Cipe's sister] in Brooklyn, and Regine turned out the chopped chicken liver and the entire meal. They did that really for their older brother, who had preceded them to the U.S. and who took Jewish holidays very seriously. For Passover, the foods were served in the proper order and there was the reading and he did that. Regine's son would sit at an angle so he could roll his eyes. For everyone else, it was a family event but not a religious event. After both of her brothers died, we got together and the chopped liver continued, but there wasn't any ceremony to it."

By the time we left, it was clear we all held a deep interest in sharing Cipe's life and legacy with the wider world. Carol gave us permission to reproduce the paintings we'd purchased in a published book, and promised to help us however she could as we pieced together the stories behind them.

Wendy and I headed back to the West Coast energized by our encounter with so many physical remnants of Cipe's life and the world she inhabited. We told friends and colleagues about her, finding time and again that even those deeply involved in the art and design worlds had never heard of her. We discovered an excellent biography, written by Martha Scotford, on which we relied greatly for our early learning about Cipe. And upon a visit to the Rochester Institute of Technology, we found a wealth of her life's work sitting in the archives, waiting to be catalogued. One day her name finally rang a bell in a conversation Wendy had with *New York Times* art director Alexandra Zsigmond. Alexandra told Wendy she'd learned of Cipe while studying at Parsons (where Cipe had taught for twenty-five years), when an undergraduate classmate was researching her, but Alexandra remembered little of the resulting report. Upon looking up Cipe anew, Alexandra discovered, as Wendy had, that her own work as an art director had incredible commonalities with Cipe's. At the *New York Times*, Alexandra makes a great effort to hire fine artists for illustration assignments. This echoes Cipe's efforts to work with fine artists when publishing fiction pieces in *Seventeen* magazine. Alexandra hadn't realized she was treading a path that Cipe had forged in editorial design, but when she looked at Cipe's work, there was no question of her influence. She remarked to Wendy, "Maybe Cipe is my spirit animal."

And that is the feeling we all seem to be left with—that this woman, whose work we'd never seen, whose name we'd never heard, nevertheless shaped how we draw, design and even exist as women. This is the history of so many women, people of color, and underrepresented groups who have been left out of the narrative, forgotten with time, but who impacted the trajectory of their fields so substantially that we wouldn't be who we are without them. Cipe's story adds a branch to our creative family tree. She is the artistic great-grandmother we never knew we had.

5

C ipe Pineles was the first independent female graphic designer in America, the first female member of the prestigious Art Directors Club, and the first woman inducted into the Art Directors Club Hall of Fame. A quarter century would pass before another woman was inducted, months before Pineles's death. Pineles was posthumously awarded the lifetime achievement medal from the American Institute of Graphic Arts, the Nobel Prize of design. And yet through all of her acclaim, Pineles was animated not by ego but by a tremendous generosity of spirit. She saw her success as belonging not to her alone but to all the women whom she was pulling up the ranks along with her, to the young designers whose lives and worlds she shaped as an educator and mentor, and to the American public, whose taste she subtly and systematically refined through the unfaltering vision that defined her life's work.

BECOMING CIPE: OUTSIDERDOM AND PERSEVERANCE
MARIA POPOVA

When I first heard of Cipe Pineles, I thought of her counterpart Maria Mitchell—a pioneer no less trailblazing in opening up an entire world of possibility to women, yet no less lamentably forgotten.

One sweltering July afternoon, I found myself stunned before one particular object at the birthplace of Maria Mitchell—America's first woman astronomer—on the small island of Nantucket. In the nineteenth century, Mitchell paved the way for women in science and became the first woman employed by the United States Federal Government for a nonspecialized domestic skill—she was hired as "computer of Venus" for the United States Nautical Almanac, performing complex mathematical computations to guide sailors around the world. She was also the first woman elected into the American Academy of Arts and Sciences. It would be another ninety years until the second woman—legendary anthropologist Margaret Mead—was admitted. The item that stopped my stride, hanging humbly in the hallway of Mitchell's small Quaker home, was her certificate of admission into the Academy. On it, the salutation "Sir" was crossed out in pencil and "honorary member" was handwritten over the printed "Fellow." This yellowing piece of paper was the fossil of a quiet, monumental revolution—the record of an opening hand-etched into a glass ceiling centuries thick.

Like Mitchell's, Pineles's path to success was neither straight nor free of obstacles.

Born to Orthodox Jewish parents in Vienna at the end of Europe's last untroubled decade before the horrors of the World Wars forever scarred the face of the Old World, young Ciporah—who soon became Cipe and never looked back—grew up as the second youngest child in a family of five, with two sisters and two older brothers. In search of relief for her father's diabetes more than a decade before the first insulin injection saved a human life, Cipe and her family migrated across Europe's most venerated spas and sanatoria before settling in

Cipe and her sisters, Regine and Debora, circa 1915

7

Poland, right outside Warsaw. (How tempting to imagine young Cipe crossing paths, without ever knowing it, with some of Europe's intellectual titans who frequented the continent's spas around the same time, seeking cures for their own bodily bedevilments—Rainer Maria Rilke, Hermann Hesse, Franz Kafka.)

From a young age, flavor and color were married for Cipe. One of her earliest memories was of walking in the woods with her siblings, gathering strawberries—"red caps through the green grass"—and sitting down by the river to savor them. In childhood, as in her professional life decades later, she was also unafraid of a difficult and even dangerous climb to the top. She recounted one particularly memorable hike in the mountains on the border between Poland and the area then known as Bohemia, on which she and her siblings had chosen one of the highest and most formidable peaks to climb. "With great difficulties after falling a few times we reached at last the top," she wrote—a sentence of inadvertent prescience as an existential allegory for her later life in the creative world.

But the adventurous idyll was violently interrupted by the outbreak of World War I. Shortly after Russia's Red Army invaded Poland in 1920, twelve-year-old Cipe and her family returned to Vienna. Years later, as a high school senior in America, she won a national essay contest by the *Atlantic* for her vivid eyewitness account of the Bolshevik-inflicted tumult in Europe, which she described as a time of "suspense, excitement, and uncertainty."

Back in Vienna, the Pineles sisters had set about learning English by memorizing Charles Dickens's *A Christmas Carol*—a strategy with a serendipitous payoff when they finally arrived in America in mid-October of 1923 ("a very beautiful day," Cipe recalled of the morning she first glimpsed the Statue of Liberty) and entered school just before the holidays, impressing classmates with their season-appropriate vocabulary. "From the beginning we have hard work," she wrote shortly after arriving, "but I think that in a few months, when we will speak and understand more English it will be much easier."

So began Pineles's life in America as a prototypical immigrant, marked by the peculiar, if lonely-making, privilege of being in a culture but not of it. "There accrue to the outsider great benefits," wrote the trailblazing biochemist Erwin Chargaff—a compatriot and contemporary of Pineles's, who immigrated to America around the same time and for similar reasons. The European sensibility she had unconsciously absorbed in her formative years would later bring to her design work a level of originality and sophistication that rose above her American peers.

At the end of her senior year of high school, classmates wrote alongside her yearbook portrait: "She knows she draws well. A little Polish girl who won our hearts." She was voted "best natured member" of her graduating class—a title that reflected the core values of kindness and generosity that never left her, even as she ascended the rungs of the corporate world in the golden age of unfeeling self-actualization.

During her final year of high school, Cipe received a fifty-dollar art scholarship—a non-negligible sum that covered more than a third of the annual art school tuition at Pratt, where she enrolled in the fall of 1926. Her graduation portfolio at Pratt was strewn with food paintings, from a loaf of bread to a chocolate cake. It was also an ode to her first big love, watercolor. Once again, a sort of character summary by her classmates appeared next to her senior portrait: "The most remarkable water colorist in our class. Boys, it's too late: Cipe is wedded to her art—and they're both happy."

"Boys, it's too late: Cipe is wedded to her art—and they're both happy."

Beneath the tongue-in-cheek remark lay a deeper truth about Cipe's attitude toward art and marriage—one nurtured by her older brother Sam, who was instrumental in encouraging her vocational autonomy. Before Pratt, she had voiced to him her reservation that attending college would keep her from finding a husband to support her. Sam reportedly replied: "Marriage is not a full-time occupation. Did you ever hear of a doctor or a lawyer giving up his profession because he was getting married?" (That her youngest sister became a doctor in an era when the field was almost entirely male is probably not coincidental.) In another conversation, Sam reiterated the sentiment: "Marriage is not a substitute for having something to do in life." Pineles did eventually get married—twice—but although she was a classic Jewish mother in some ways, including in the kitchen, she never let her family life contract her expansive devotion to her art.

Pineles's name worked both for and against her. To the American ear, Cipe Pineles bears a peculiar ambiguity. An ambiguous foreign name functions like the screen behind which orchestra auditions are performed—the applicant's gender, ethnicity, age, and other potential points of bias are obscured to let the music speak for itself. But unlike orchestras, which employ

9

this strategy deliberately to avoid bias, the magazine world of mid-century America had no such noble commitment to impartiality. The screen of Cipe Pineles's name was accidental and as soon as her gendered identity was revealed, the opportunities dwindled or disappeared altogether. She would later recount: "I would drop my portfolio off at various advertising agencies. But the people who liked my work and were interested enough to ask me in for an interview had assumed by my name that I was a man! When they finally met me, they were disappointed, and I left the interview without a chance for the job." Some prospective employers explained that if she were hired, she'd have to work in the bullpen—an enormous corporate hangar of men—where a woman's presence would be ill-advised and downright unwelcome.

Still, she pressed on. Reluctantly, she took a job as a watercolor teacher at New Jersey's Newark Public School of Fine and Industrial Art in the fall of 1929, at a salary of ten dollars a week, but she continued to search for work in the commercial world. Compounding the persistent gender obstacle was the inopportune timing of cultural catastrophe: Pineles had graduated from Pratt just before the devastating stock market crash of 1929 and was attempting to enter the workforce at the dawn of the Great Depression.

Determined to succeed, she scoured the New York Public Library for a list of advertising agencies working with food accounts, purposefully pursuing her passion for the intersection of food and graphic art.

She was eventually hired by Contempora—the experimental consortium of designers, artists, and architects including Lucian Bernhard, Paul Poiret, Rockwell Kent, and others—where she designed fabric and dimensional displays. But her real breakthrough came obliquely to her direct efforts. The magazine magnate Condé Nast saw her pattern design and window fabric displays for Contempora. They were unlike anything Nast had seen. He immediately hired Pineles as an editorial designer for *Vogue* and *Vanity Fair*, both of which she imprinted with her singular vision. She continued to move up in the magazine world. By the mid-1940s, she was shaping the visual voice of *Glamour* and earning the magazine every prestigious accolade of design.

> "Eating is more than food . . . it is visual impact, contrast, style, scale, mood, fragrance, color."

10

It was in this period that she began illustrating *Leave Me Alone with the Recipes*, perhaps because she was contending for the first time with negotiating the competing roles of traditional womanhood and a thriving corporate career, which she followed to the very top over the next half-century, eventually pouring the confluence of her accomplished expertise and her generosity of spirit into teaching as well. She became a passionate and beloved educator at Parsons, where she taught editorial design for nearly two decades.

Exactly thirty years after she wrote and illustrated her family cookbook, Pineles had a chance to resurrect her love of the intersection of the culinary and graphic arts. In 1975—a tumultuous year for her, marked by her induction into the Art Directors Club Hall of Fame and the sudden death of her lover—she spearheaded the Parsons yearbook project, themed "cheap eats": a collection of illustrated recipes for delicious but affordable meals by students, faculty, and celebrated artists such as Maurice Sendak, Larry Rivers, and Elaine de Kooning. Alongside an original painting, Pineles herself contributed a recipe for kasha served with meatballs, a version of which appears in *Leave Me Alone with the Recipes*.

The students' introduction to the yearbook encapsulated Pineles's influence as an educator, artist, and cross-pollinator of food and design, and it captured the spirit and sensibility of her unpublished 1945 family cookbook with uncanny precision. They wrote: "The style is in the color, the scale, the original and unusual use of common items and of art materials. The recipes and ideas in this cookbook are made with the same ingredients any student on a budget would buy; but it is the resourcefulness and inventiveness as well as the artists' love for cooking which make for good design and especially creative meals. Eating is more than food . . . it is visual impact, contrast, style, scale, mood, fragrance, color."

Visual impact, indeed, was the raw material of Pineles's work. But from it radiated a larger legacy of cultural impact. A century earlier, to her first class of female astronomers at Vassar, Maria Mitchell had remarked, "No woman should say, 'I am but a woman!' But a woman! What more can you ask to be?" Pineles's life and legacy were one quiet but continuous incarnation of this incantation, the reverberations of which live on as the palpable pulse animating the corpus of possibility for every contemporary woman in publishing and graphic design.

11

FOOD & DRINK

SARAH RICH

In the early 1960s, Cipe decided to more formally and fully incorporate her love of food into her magazine work by launching a new publication entitled *Food & Drink*. At the time, *Gourmet* magazine had been in print for twenty years, but it, along with the few other titles in the same category, targeted female homemakers. In contrast, *Food & Drink* would be for both men and women; it would not only be instructional but investigative and intellectual, looking at gastronomy through the eyes of some of the greatest writers of that era. The list of planned contributors included Marianne Moore, Eudora Welty, Pierre Salinger, Clifton Fadiman, and Erich Fromm in addition to food greats like M.F.K. Fisher, Elizabeth David, and Craig Claiborne. The editorial team was to be led by James Beard, along with Helen McCully, who had been the food editor at *McCall's* and *House Beautiful*; Tracy Samuels, a *Better Living* magazine editor and playwright; and Cipe, whose credits at that point included *Seventeen*, *Charm*, *Mademoiselle*, *Vogue*, and others.

The team had the support of Richard V. Benson, a wealthy direct-mail advertising magnate who had founded *American Heritage* magazine and helped start *Smithsonian*. His introductory letter to *Food & Drink* began, "Dear Bon Vivants . . . From our ancestors' primitive foraging for nuts and berries and wild boar, gastronomy has become one of man's most fascinating and complex occupations. Yet, until now, there has never been a magazine which examined this field regularly, comprehensively, engagingly."

The editorial team made an extra effort to emphasize men's potential interest in the magazine, since it could be taken for granted that women would gravitate toward it. Another teaser for the publication, written by Beard, began, "We men like to read about food and drink as much as women do. Maybe more. But we haven't exactly been encouraged to take a good romp through fine eating territory on the printed page. Most of the material published in magazines seems to be aimed exclusively at women. And only at certain kinds of women, at that. It's coy and cute. Or frilly. Or dull. Or long-winded. Or meandering, with recipes as leaven for otherwise flighty essays. High time all that was changed, in our opinion. And changed it is, with the first issue of *Food & Drink*, the new magazine for the inner man."

Cipe's archives, housed at the Rochester Institute of Technology, include typed and hand-sketched pages for the first few issues of the magazine. Volume 1 was set to include a piece from mystery writer Rex Stout entitled "Nero Wolfe Cooks an Orchid" (Wolfe being the fictional protagonist of Stout's many detective novels). Another essay asked, "Is Speed Killing Our Cuisine?" and was to be assigned to M.F.K. Fisher. "Dinner Party at our Embassy in Gabon," would be written by Mrs. Charles Darlington, the wife of a diplomat stationed in central Africa in the 1960s. To keep things culinary, Julia Child would contribute "The Endless Possibilities of a Properly Poached Chicken," and Craig Claiborne, the famed *New York Times* food writer, was writing "Chefs Don't Eat What You Eat." In the "service" section, the list of pieces included "Is Your Blender Sitting on Its Hands?", "The Hot Banana," and "Sour Cream: The Suave Touch."

If *Food & Drink* had been born in the late 2000s, it almost certainly would have been *Lucky Peach*—a masculine-leaning, irreverent, bold-voiced magazine. Like *Lucky Peach*, it wanted to win its audience by running counter to what was expected of a publication in its sector. But it was the 1960s, and for whatever reason, a concept that seemed so smart, edgy, and broadly appealing never took off. Perhaps it was due to Benson's plan to keep the magazine off newsstands and available only by mail to subscribers. Perhaps it was something else. In Cipe's archives, there is a single-page typed letter from *Food & Drink*'s president and publisher, James B. Horton, addressed to the magazine's investors. "Food & Drink, Inc., having no assets, is now considered an abandoned Corporation," he wrote, "You will notice that we had a cash balance of $109.79 in 1963. This amount has been expended during the year 1964 on legal fees."

With that tiny financial consideration accounted for, the promising venture dissolved, its amazing potential stored in a time capsule in Cipe's files. Horton went on to launch *Food & Wine* magazine in the 1970s while acting as VP at Playboy Enterprises, but as we know, it fell in line as a magazine primarily for women, home cooks, and entertainers. Today we have a few other titles that conjure the spirit of *Food & Drink*, but one can only imagine what that publication would be now, had it come to life and endured for the next half century.

13

PAULA SCHER

AN EVENING WITH ONE OF THE BEST

I learned who Cipe Pineles was when I was in my twenties and first married to Seymour Chwast. She had been an art director of *Charm* and *Mademoiselle* at Condé Nast, as well as *Seventeen*. Seymour had won a competition and had his first published illustration in *Seventeen* while she was art director there. I had learned from Seymour that Cipe was a powerful woman, art director, and designer, and that she had been married to both the designers Will Burtin and Bill Golden. Cipe was the first female member of the Art Directors Club (it was really a "club" in those days) and she was inducted into their Hall of Fame in 1975. She was also one of the very few woman members of Alliance Graphic International.

In 1964, I started a design firm with a friend named Terry Koppel called Koppel and Scher. I had become active in AIGA and had begun writing ad hoc articles in the *AIGA Journal*. I had written a very snarky article about the state of recent magazine design at Condé Nast entitled "The Mystery of Conde Nasty," in which I ranted about their stupid scrapbook style that used ripped paper and photos that were overlaid with nonsensical writing and giant pull-quotes. The piece appeared in the second or third issue of the tabloid-size *AIGA Journal of Graphic Design*. About a week after it appeared, I got a call at Koppel and Scher from Cipe Pineles. She loved the Condé Nasty piece, said she laughed out loud, and invited me over to her apartment for dinner.

I was surprised by the invitation and took her up on it, but I really didn't know what to expect. When I arrived at her apartment, I found it would be just the two of us. We made some light chit chat about her apartment, Condé Nasty, my design business, the AIGA, and Parsons School of Design, where she was a department chair. Then she brought me into her kitchen, sat me down at a table and made us each a hamburger on a bun. After she finished eating, she abruptly got up, went into another room and came back with some poster or mailer in her hand. "And what do you think of this?" she asked defiantly.

It was a mailer that I had already seen for a lecture series to be held at the Art Directors Club. The poster had a black and white photo of ten or more white men, all on individual chairs, seated in a group. The headline over the picture said, "An Evening with One of the Best." Some of the men in the picture were George Lois, Henry Wolf, Lou Dorfsman, Gene Federico, and then there were advertising guys whose names I don't remember. But the bunch of men in the group were designers and art directors that I used to call "the machers," which is Yiddish for "big shot."

"Would you look at them!" Cipe said. "Not even one token woman. Not even a lousy woman designer that they all like socially!" I began laughing because it was absurd and seemingly pointless. Not all of the men were even anywhere near "the best." They were just a social group.

We began planning our own evening lecture series called "An Evening with Ones with Big Breasts," or some such thing, and the conversation devolved into hilarity, but the point was made and for that moment, we bonded. Later that evening, I realized that she was very hurt by the pathetic exclusion in that silly ADC program, and I would feel that same hurt for the same silly exclusions many, many times after.

She used her outrage as a bridge to form an alliance with me, and surely with many other talented but marginalized women. Her rejection of the male-dominated structure of the publishing and design industries helped move things in the direction of equality, and while things are not perfect today, women's leadership is growing. Cipe was unwilling to be ignored and she couldn't be; her work had its own voice, and it compelled people to listen.

15

Photo of Cipe at work by
Ed Feingersh

These days, most cookbooks are filled cover to cover with lush, spectacular, highly produced photographs intended to inspire the reader and present a goal for the home cook to achieve. However beautiful these photos are, they can also feel intimidating and un-attainable—almost too perfect. Immaculately arranged and styled, these cookbook photos often feel more like they're about lighting, digital pixels, and Photoshop than about making something with your hands in a home kitchen. Cooking is something you do with your eyes, your ears, your nose. You use all your senses to prepare a delicious dish. Given the personal, tactile nature of preparing food, you'd think a cookbook would visually convey how it looks, feels, and tastes to make something—how it feels to, you know, *cook*.

Cooking was never really my thing. But eating and drawing was. Maybe I first started drawing coffee. More likely it was wine. Whatever it was it was sitting in front of me, and being someone who drew whatever was in front of me, I became rather adept at drawing the loopy lines of a late night with good friends and a couple bottles of booze. When I ate out or traveled I'd pull out my sketchbook at the table and draw any food that struck my fancy; anything that seemed unusual in color, arrangement, or taste. Soon I

17

WENDY MACNAUGHTON IN DEFENSE OF FOOD ILLUSTRATION

was drawing for food-related magazines—*Food & Wine*, *Lucky Peach*, *Edible San Francisco*—and slowly I started to become known as an illustrator who draws food. But really I was just an illustrator who likes to draw and eat. I was no chef, but I was developing a palette, both in flavor and in paint. The more I drew, the more I appreciated the architecture of a pomegranate exploded across a counter, the pattern of a herringbone tart with the edges of its apples browned and settling into puffing frangipane. The more I drew, the more I noticed. A salad was no longer just a mess of green, it was a mixture of emerald, olive, and pine, bursts of cranberry with bits of subtle creams and blues peeking through. Sometimes I would draw a plate spilling over with beautiful food, only to draw the plate again, post-dinner, representing its irresistibility through the crumbs left.

Illustration can convey a love of food and aesthetic in a deeply personal, sensual, accessible way that other mediums just cannot. It's what Cipe Pineles did in her cookbook in the 1940s. And it's what many people are getting back to doing now. To some this might feel like the introduction of a new style. It's not. Illustration and hand-lettering have been used in cookbooks as far back as the seventeenth century. It was terribly time consuming and expensive to create these pictures back then, so the black-and-white step-by-step instructions were a rare treat to find tucked in between the hand-set pages. As printing processes improved, so did cookbook illustrations. Simple black-and-white cross sections of how to carve meat, fish, and chicken became lush hand-colored etchings, then eventually four-color lithography. The first full-color cookbook was printed around the late eighteenth century, and the illustrations were as much about depicting a lifelike, beautiful dish as they were about showing the reader how to make it.

Then photography came along and replaced drawing as the way to represent reality. In the case of cookbooks, this meant finished dishes and table settings started to be demonstrated through photographs, and illustration was relegated back to instruction or used as some simple visual garnish. As photography got cheaper to produce and reproduce, it replaced illustration as the primary language of cookbooks. Think of all those 1960s cookbooks with their pages packed with photos. By then, illustration had been nearly pushed completely off the page. Then digital photography was introduced. Then the Internet. Enter food porn and websites filled with food photography. Then Instagram. You get where I'm going. And that pretty much takes us up to today.

Of course, there've been some notable exceptions along the way. A handful of beautiful, illustrated cookbooks you're likely to have on your bookshelf were created during the rise of photography. James Beard's *Fireside Cookbook* (1949) with artwork by the Provensens is a study in the joy and

18

storytelling that illustration can achieve. *Mastering the Art of French Cooking* (1961) by Julia Child, illustrated by Sidonie Coryn, is a classic. Amy Vanderbilt's *Complete Cookbook* (1961) continued the tradition of black-and-white line drawing instructions created by a little-known-at-the-time illustrator named Andy Warhol. The 1964 edition of *The Joy of Cooking*, by Irma S. Rombauer and Marion Rombauer Becker, was illustrated cover to cover by Ginnie Hoffman and Beverly Warner. And *Moosewood Cookbook* (1977) was both written and illustrated by Molly Katzen.

And tucked deep within these exceptions to the photographic rule, hidden in an attic away from public sight, was Cipe Pineles's unpublished cookbook *Leave Me Alone with the Recipes*—a 100-percent hand-drawn, expertly painted, perfectly imperfectly hand-lettered cookbook of family recipes drawn directly into a hardcover sketchbook. Part recipe, part memoir, part painting practice and hand-lettering exercise, *Leave Me Alone with the Recipes* is a study in what illustration can achieve. In her personal cookbook, Cipe draws like a great chef cooks. You can see the years of study. Her skill is clear. And precisely because of this high level of craft, she's able to riff with her paints, combine unlikely elements of color and letter, be loose and spontaneous with her layout. Cipe's love of food, history, and art comes through in every drawn recipe, on every page. Her drawings, lettering, and composition are far from perfect, but everything always ends up looking just right.

Artwork made by hand connects with readers in a way a photograph cannot. It reads as human and accessible. You can see right there on the page the time and care that went into the drawing's creation. In turn, looking at it can demand some time and care from the viewer. Handmadeness slows people down. It creates a connection between the artist and the viewer. In food illustration, not only do you see the subject, but you can get a sense of the movements and attitude of the person behind the art and the joy with which the drawing was made. Just as when people say you can taste when food was made with love, you can also see when a drawing was made with love.

Cipe's *Leave Me Alone with the Recipes* and other illustrated cookbooks in its genre (yes, let's state it—this is a genre!) takes us back to a time when there were no computers. There were no microwaves or fast food. There was no Photoshop. Instead, there was a long tradition of drawing and painting. There was attention, care, and play. There was time and there was practice. And you could see that in every cookbook illustration—in Cipe's and beyond. In our automated, tech-filled, efficient lives, hand-drawn illustration gets us to think about process. To remember the things that only humans

Cipe draws like a great chef cooks }

19

can create—in art, in design, and in the kitchen. Hand-drawn illustration in cookbooks brings us back to our most basic senses. And it does what Cipe's cookbook does for me as an illustrator—it helps us remember from whence we came.

ON BRAND

DEBBIE MILLMAN

When I started in the brand design industry in 1992, I was struck by the lack of women in senior positions in the business. I was working for a company then called The Schechter Group (now Interbrand), which was founded by Alvin Schechter several decades before. Our competitors were firms such as Wallace Church, Gerstman + Meyers, and, of course, Landor. All of these companies had tremendous reputations, and all—*every single one*—were founded and run by men. As a newly minted business development executive, my job was to call on consumer goods companies for their business. In doing so, I found that the corporate design directors in senior positions were *also* men. There was nary a woman to be found. The graphic design business fared slightly better back then, but just barely. Paula Scher had recently become the first female partner at Pentagram, and for a brief moment, designer and brand strategist Cheryl Heller was a partner at Frankfurt Gips Balkind. But for the most part, if a woman wanted to be at the helm of a design firm, she had to start her own agency. But that didn't always work, either: when Charles and Ray Eames jointly ran their eponymous business, Ray often played second fiddle to her more famous husband (assuming she wasn't mistakenly referred to as Charles's *brother* Ray, rather than his spouse). The stewardship of the brand and graphic design communities represented this state of affairs accurately: in its first one hundred years, AIGA, the professional association for design, elected only four women to preside over the largest design organization in the world. And despite a mission of "championing the very best in commercial creativity," it took the Art Directors Club fifty-five years to allow *any* woman to become a member.

That woman was Cipe Pineles. The year was 1948, and despite repeated nominations from well-known ADC members, she was continually denied membership to the venerable organization. When the ADC invited Pineles's husband, CBS designer William Golden, to join, he refused and emphatically stated that the ADC could not be considered a "serious, professional organization if it would not admit his wife, a well-qualified, award-winning art director for many years." According to Martha Scotford's biography of Pineles, the club extended an invitation to both Golden and Pineles the next day; they both immediately accepted.

Cipe Pineles's success was often hard-won. A young immigrant growing up in Brooklyn, New York, Pineles showed an early affinity and talent in art. Despite numerous accolades and awards while studying at Pratt Institute (including earning one of sixteen scholarships available during her senior year) and winning a fellowship to the Louis Comfort Tiffany Foundation, Cipe spent over a year after her graduation searching for a job.

Cipe found her first position in graphic design at Green Mansions, the adult resort and summer camp in the Adirondack Mountains of upstate New York, and at Contempora, Ltd, an association of European and American artists and designers, before being hired at Condé Nast under the esteemed head of design, Dr. Mehemed Fehmy Agha.

Cipe Pineles spent fourteen years at Condé Nast, first assisting and learning from Dr. Agha at *Vogue, Vanity Fair,* and *House & Garden.* She honed her skills in typography, photo editing, collage, page layout, and art direction. She was appointed art director of *Glamour* in 1941 and began to experiment with a signature style. Cipe quickly applied her uniquely inquisitive eye with a distinct creative elegance and transformed the magazine. Her illustrative flair, confidence with white space, and her witty, joyful use of materials created an utterly unmistakable visual language for *Glamour.* Through these years, she developed the holistic, multidisciplinary perspective that one needs in order to bring a brand to life.

In late 1946 Cipe was invited by former Condé Nast colleague Helen Valentine to join her at a magazine she had recently launched. Titled *Seventeen,* the magazine was the first ever to treat and appeal to teenagers as exuberant young adults. By 1948, Cipe was appointed art director and was given free rein to create the visual essence of the publication in its entirety. She began to invite fine artists to create illustrations for the magazine and stated, "To label art that is printed as 'commercial' has done and is doing an enormous amount of damage to artists and to everyone in the Graphic Arts. This label has kept some great talent away from us." Cipe invited artists such as Andy Warhol, Carol Blanchard, Louis Bouché, Alexander Brook, Jacob Lawrence, Karl Zerbe, and many, many others to contribute to *Seventeen* and the vibrancy, vitality, and unique cultural voice elevated the new publication to become one of the most successful launches in magazine history, even to this day.

In 1950 Cipe transitioned to become the art director of *Charm* magazine, a new publication for "women who work." Not content to appeal to "the girl behind the typewriter," the magazine set out to help the "girl just out of school, get her first job . . . and balance her time and energies between home and office." Cipe's work on *Charm* was nothing short of a tour de force. Her skills as a photography editor and typographer were miraculous: elegant but approachable, dignified but whimsical. It is during this time—in her third major role at a publishing house—that Cipe became more than an art director with a great eye and a superb hand with typography. At *Charm*, Cipe came into her own as a master brand designer. During Cipe's tenure at *Charm*, she proved that her talents defining the visual equities of a brand weren't based on her personal style or individual point of view. She could create singular worlds readers could effortlessly enter and be enveloped by. She created deliberate, differentiated brand personalities with individual traits and values and beliefs. And each—especially *Charm*—were imbued with an integrity designed by someone with more than mere "design" talent. Cipe Pineles used the very foundation of branding—positioning—to understand and appeal to a variety of disparate, fundamentally different audiences. That each effort resulted in resounding success has as much to do with her talent as a designer as it does her talent as a cultural anthropologist, behavioral psychologist, economist, and marketer. In short, Cipe Pineles was a brand consultant before the discipline was even invented.

"To label art that is printed as 'commercial' . . . has kept some great talent away from us."

Beginning in 1961, Cipe joined her second husband, Will Burtin, in his design consultancy. There she was commissioned by clients including Lincoln Center, AIGA, *Print* magazine, the Russell Sage Foundation, the Museum of Early American Folk Arts, and *Ladies' Home Journal*. She crafted logos, brochures and publications, posters, calendars, and magazine illustrations. She also began an entirely new phase of her career: academia. In 1962, Cipe began teaching at Parsons School of Design, and in 1970 she took on the additional mantle of Parsons' Director of Publications. There, she educated and worked with students and staff to remake the college's many books, brochures, and posters. And once again, Cipe brought a unique personality and verve to the materials that not only captured the imagi-

23

nation of the student body, they—like any successful brand expression—helped clarify and define the school's mission, vision, and values to the public.

Over her long and illustrious career, Cipe Pineles not only broke new ground as a woman in design, she also singlehandedly injected the art and discipline of branding into the rarefied worlds of publishing and education. Without ever knowing it, Cipe Pineles made it possible for designers, artists, editors, and entrepreneurs including Martha Stewart, Ina Garten, Anna Wintour, Tavi Gevinson, Iris Apfel, Heidi Klum, Kate Bingaman-Burt, Jessica Hische, Sophie Blackall, hundreds of male *and* female brand consultants, and millions of bloggers, writers, and stylists working today to follow in her footsteps and create or invigorate brands based on the use of innovative visual language. Despite her death in 1991, the exquisitely timeless work of Cipe Pineles continues to inspire designers from every genre to invent beautiful new visual worlds, and still profoundly inspires us all to want to live in them.

C ipe Pineles was a rare individual the likes of whom may never be seen again. I'll spare the superlatives, except to say that she helped shape modern graphic and periodical design in the United States. Petite and refined, with an Old World Austrian lilt to her speech, she maintained a joyful yet fatalistic sense of humor that came through her work. Unlike some of her more heavily accented, émigré male modernist counterparts who used the English language like a sledgehammer, Pineles's soothing timbre added to an exotic yet masterful personal and influential directing style when working with artists and photographers.

DESIGN PIONEER STEVEN HELLER

The exquisite quality of her art direction during the 1930s, '40s, and '50s of *Glamour*, *Overseas Woman*, *Seventeen*, and *Charm* was equal to if not better than that of many of the great men of that time. Talent alone did not ensure jobs: women could paper their walls with rejection letters. But in 1933 while assisting the eminent Dr. M. F. Agha, art director of Condé Nast's *Vanity Fair* and *Vogue*, she received an enviable education.

"We used to make many versions of the same feature," Cipe once told me. "If we did, let's say, twenty pages on beauty with twenty different photographers, we made scores of different layouts in order to extract every bit of drama or humor we could out of that material." This experience taught her a valuable lesson that magazine design should never play second fiddle to advertising.

After apprenticing with Agha, she was promoted to art director at *Glamour*, a poor relation to *Vogue*, targeted to women who couldn't afford high-priced fashion. In 1944 she took over *Overseas Woman*, an army magazine for American servicewomen stationed abroad, which she handled with style and taste. Then the best of jobs came her way.

Seventeen magazine. For the first time in American commercial history this monthly created a market genre, indeed an entire segment of the population that did not exist, called teenage girls. Before this, male and female teenagers were relegated to a netherworld between childhood and adulthood (think Andy Hardy). Cipe was empowered to visually chart new territory that would ultimately alter social habits forever.

Art direction was greater than its parts—more than routine layout or picture selection: Cipe chose the models and developed the atmosphere in which garments, accessories—the entire gestalt of the new teenage girl was presented. Believing the magazine's readers were thoughtful beings rather than attention-deficient automatons, Cipe introduced editorial illustration that pushed away from typically saccharine *Saturday Evening Post* vignettes to expressive and interpretive art. She proudly told me: "I avoided illustration that was weighed down by cliche´ or conventions." Rather than force her artists to mimic the text, Pineles allowed them to paint what they *felt*. She also urged *Seventeen*'s fashion photographers to make the models "look normal." Typography was not formulaic either, but rather designed according to the same expressive mandates as illustration, which gave her layouts a timeless quality, even by today's standards. "Most important is the talent to harness it and create momentum so that the reader will keep turning the pages," she told me.

Cipe cherished her relationship with Parsons School of Design, and created dozens of her own watercolor and gouache illustrations, like the ones in this book, for the school's promotional publications. To be close to Parsons she kept a small Manhattan apartment on 9th Street between University Place and Broadway, only a few blocks away from the school. It was there that I saw her last.

When I was art director of the *New York Times Book Review*, Cipe invited me to critique the final projects of her Parsons magazine design class. Of course, it was an honor. They were juniors or seniors, perhaps with graduation on their minds, and so I was surprised by the lack of interest her students seemed to have taking classes headed by such a preeminent figure. They did the work, but there was something lackadaisical about their respective presentations. It was the late '80s, so magazines were not dead yet and I was disappointed in some of the results. They should have appreciated the living history in their midst, even if their tastes and preferences were generationally different.

After class, Cipe and I returned to the 9th Street apartment, where I

26

expressed frustration with their energy levels. She assured me that there were some very talented kids in the class. Magnanimity was Cipe's greatest personal contribution to the world of design. Magnanimity showed in her dedication and love of teaching others. She was various parts conductor and catalyst using her own experience not as a template but as an example to follow, modify, or reject.

Graphic design history is not made in a vacuum—there are great makers, superb directors, and inspiring teachers. Cipe was all three and indeed a pioneer in a profession that had yet to experience its overwhelming demographic shift. She vehemently objected to the idea that being a woman who broke down barriers was an accomplishment on which to hang her legacy. Rather it was just a part of a larger career. I know if she were still alive we would nonetheless agree to differ.

Cipe on a design jury. Photographer and date unknown.

27

COOK UNTIL IT LOOKS RIGHT

MIMI SHERATON

Editors' note: As soon as we had her sketchbook in hand in early 2013, we began looking for people who'd known Cipe professionally or socially. Fortunately for us, we were able to reach a person whose value to this project went far beyond simply having known Cipe. Mimi Sheraton was born about twenty years after Cipe to a Jewish family that hailed from a similar region of Eastern Europe. Both their families had settled in Brooklyn and both women, after leaving college, entered the New York publishing world.

Like Cipe, Mimi eventually wrote a book chronicling her mother's recipes, which she published in 1977. From My Mother's Kitchen features recipes for almost every dish included in Cipe's sketchbook, plus many more. Their culinary and cultural traditions were a matched set.

In 1949 Mimi joined the editorial staff at **Seventeen** *magazine, where Cipe was art director. And although Mimi has become a legend in her own right since that time, she still holds onto richly detailed memories of the woman who presided over art and design at one of her first magazine jobs— the way Cipe wore her hair, the foods she spoke of hungrily and served generously, and the power she wielded when arguing for a layout.*

At age twenty-three, I arrived at *Seventeen* after a year at the very staid *Good Housekeeping*. I was hired as home furnishings editor and three years later became food editor as well. What struck me was the unfettered, young, and innovative staff and spirit at *Seventeen*, then a fairly new magazine—maybe six years old—strictly for high school teenage girls.

In those days at *Seventeen*, the editors wore formal clothes and always hats in the office (but not Cipe). Young staff and junior editors dressed ballet-ish, with ponytails, loose dirndl skirts, tight sort of ballet T-shirts, and always Capezio ballet-like flat slippers, especially in the art department, where they all brought in odd and beautiful things of all sorts and hung them or put them on bulletin boards. That made the art department my favorite place to hang out.

The openness of the editors there was a delight and none garnered more respect or awe from me than Cipe Pineles. She was so firm about art choices and developed new looks for magazine illustrations far removed from the staid sort in others, using people like David Stone Martin and, I believe, Saul Steinberg once or twice. I was somewhat intimidated by her European style, soft central European accent, and appearance—hair pulled back tightly, tiny earrings, sort of a scrubbed look with no cosmetics that I recall, though I have seen photos of her obviously made-up. She wore very simple loose clothing in muted colors and usually got her way in editorial meetings. If she did not, she could sulk and clam up pretty good. Few wanted to cross her.

Cipe was always treated tenderly by the other editors, as though she were some kind of super talented child. That did not keep them from disagreeing on editorial matters, but always tenderly; she seemed to expect that.

There were women at all of the women's magazines. All the top editors were women, with maybe one exception at *House & Garden* for a while. It was more unusual to see women on the business side than on editorial. At that time, several big department stores were run by women—Dorothy Shaver at Lord & Taylor, Mildred Custin at Bonwit Teller, later Gerry Stutz at Bendel.

At *Seventeen*, food articles consisted mostly of recipes for things to serve at parties and baking and candy recipes for holidays. Cipe as well as other editors were very much into what we now call "cucina povera," Italian for "food of the poor." They and she always talked about lentils, soups, heavy breads and, of all things, ham butts. I once went to a cocktail party at her home and recall only the usual types of pass-around canapes. On workdays, she and many other editors, including me, often had

29

lunch at Mary Elizabeth's, a bakery and lunchroom close to *Seventeen*'s first offices (11 West 42nd Street). It featured, as I recall, two or three soups of the day and bread with some pastries from the bakery famous for crullers.

Cipe's apartment at the time loomed large for all of us, as it was very photogenic and useful as a backdrop for magazine photos. Most especially, the fashion department used it when doing lingerie and sleepwear shoots. Among the home furnishings I wrote about were things to include in hope chests, if you can believe that, and so we did lots with sheets and blankets and bedspreads, which usually looked great in her bedroom. That room remains clear in my mind—a big corner room with two double white spool beds on opposite walls facing each other, covered in pieced quilts—as I recall floral patterns on white, white organdy curtains, white walls completely hung with botanical prints. The only problem was using that room too often in the magazine, but we always found an excuse to justify it. The room was so feminine, it was hard to imagine her very handsome, very masculine husband William Golden, the CBS art director, sleeping in it. The living room was dark, but one thing stands out in memory—a large, heavily carved Swiss cuckoo clock that Cipe had had completely sprayed with flat white paint—to fantastic results, like Hans Arp white-on-white gone crazy.

When I first saw Cipe's cookbook, as much as I was delighted by its charm, I suddenly felt as though I had never really known the true woman. How could someone so deep into sophisticated art, dress, food, and decor have grown up on the exact same kind of food that was in my family's tradition? Had I known that, I might have felt her more approachable, but I never heard her utter a word that would suggest any of this kind of food. My maternal grandmother came from a part of Romania via years in Poland, Austria, and Germany and learned to cook from a Hungarian neighbor when she was a young bride. I only recently learned that though born in Vienna, Cipe spent much of her childhood in Poland, so that might account for versions of recipes—and their names—that I rarely heard of outside my own circle of family and friends with parents of similar backgrounds.

When I started to test recipes with my mother for my own cookbook, and began to measure ingredients as she added them, she stopped short and asked me, "Are we going to measure or are we going to cook?" Her standard instruction to me about food preparation was "Until it looks right." Similar for Cipe's mother—after all, there is the title *Leave Me Alone with the Recipes*. These were Old World artisans who knew their craft.

Allowing for Cipe's frequent misspellings—always an "*e*" at the end of tomato and potato; "parseley," "knap" for knob celery, the ingredients matched those I was used to—for example, lots of root vegetables in chicken soup, and flanken being added. There are the sweet and sour touches I am used to in things such as stuffed peppers and stuffed cabbage, and for both, gingersnaps are additions that my mother always used toward the end, to add flavor but also to bind the sauces.

Besides the charming, typically Cipe illustrations in this book, things that also delighted me were the caraway (she uses *k*) soup that my grandmother made for breakfast and no one else ever seems to have heard of; the recipe for kasha straight from the box—Wolfe, I think is the brand; and also a term we never used for potatoes, *bulbenick*. I heard it from Russian Jews but never at our house. Potatoes were always *kartoffel*—maybe a strange difference in regional style of my grandmother in Bremen, as she used and therefore we used many German-Yiddish words instead of Eastern European Yiddish.

Probably no word surprised me more than *kalacha*—the name of a dish I do not believe I have ever seen in print elsewhere except in my own book. And we did not spell it quite the same, nor do we have exactly the same version of the dish. We used it for mock gefilte fish, as did Cipe's mother, but ours was and is ground chicken cooked and seasoned exactly as the fish would be. Cipe's version is based on beef or veal prepared that way. We called it *kalechla*—small differences but all in the ballpark. She also uses the same name for a meatloaf, so it obviously has something to do with ground meat.

As for Cipe's Giblet Fricassee, this is a dish my son requests for special occasions. In Ashkenazi food terminology, fricassee refers to the sort of dish Hungarians and Austrians knew as *paprikash*—braised with onions, garlic, black pepper, and lots of paprika, usually sweet paprika in Jewish cookery, a bit of hot in Austro-Hungarian and mine. The big difference is that Jews do not add sour cream (kosher laws) to the sauce and so come up with another product. As for giblets, nothing was thrown away, and if not used in this dish, the gizzards, necks, and hearts would be cooked in soups. Meatballs of beef with some rice were always part of this, whether with chicken or giblets—tiny ones, not usually browned but more or less cooked in the sauce as dumplings. When the fricassee was of giblets and tiny meatballs, it was a hot appetizer; with chicken, it was and is a main course. I have no thoughts on how to update these—God forbid!—they do not need modernizing but should be served in the classic way. If you worry about cholesterol, start with Lipitor.

Her standard instruction to me about food preparation was "Until it looks right."

31

MAIRA KALMAN

AN ODE TO CIPE

Editors' note: When we discovered Cipe's cookbook we immediately thought of the work of one of the great illustrators of our time, Maira Kalman. We invited her to create a reflection on Cipe's legacy.

I never met Cipe Pineles, but clearly, she was a Role Model for many. A Modern Woman. No Nonsense. With a discerning Eye. Getting things DONE with other women and men of taste and culture. Not being Afraid. Having SELF-Confidence. You Bet. Look at the bow and the watch and the TILT of the head. Get on with it and LOOK for the WIT and Beauty.

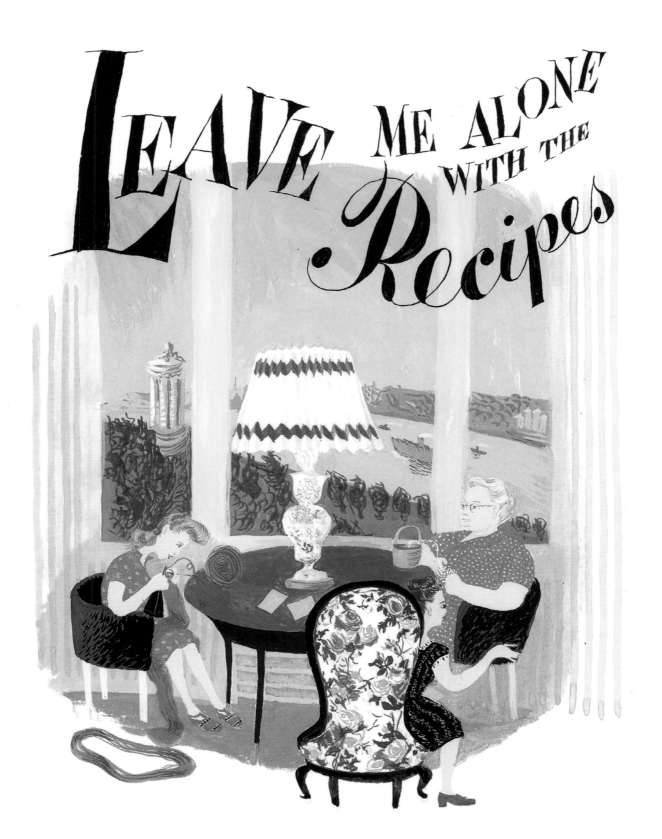

LEAVE ME ALONE WITH THE Recipes

RECIPES... Mrs. PINELES

PICTURES... CIPE PINELES

1945

Chicken soup

1. celery
1. root parseley
2. carrots
1. onion
1. leek
1. knap celery (small)
3 or 4 bones (not breast bones)
1. lb. plate or breast flanken
CHICKEN
paprica, salt, lima beans

Wash chicken in cold water; remove all insides, put into deep dish; pour boiling water over everything except gizzard, which gets cleaned in cold water. Pluck all feathers and stubbs and scrape skin clean with knife. Drain and salt inside and outside. When cold cover with waxpaper and place in icebox overnight. Cook the next day.......
Put vegetables and bones in 3 pints of cold water in covered pot. Skim foam till clear. (2 or 3 minutes). Add the whole chicken✳ Cook for about an hour (tough chicken an hour and a half) with cover a little off. Cook soup without chicken till meat is tender. Use chicken neck and feet in soup. Serve with rice, noodles, potatoes or matzo balls, always with chopped parseley.
WHEN YOU BROWN THAT CHICKEN cut a garlic and onion into a pan with chicken fat. add paprica, half a tomatoe and simmer for a while. add chicken, which has been salted and sprinkled with paprica, and roast in oven, basting frequently.

✳ whole or quartered; add hot water whenever necessary

38

BORSHT

3 bunches beets
1 onion
1 table sp. sugar
1½ lemons (juice)
2 eggs
½ pint sour cream
1 tsp. salt

Peal three bunches of beets (wear rubber gloves) and grate with medium grater into large pot. Put in large onion; add cold water, more than covering the beets. Cook one hour till beets are soft. Add sugar earlier in cooking. Add salt and lemon juice. Taste. When cool, take out onion; beat up thoroughly the eggs and mix with soup. When cold add ½ pint (or less) sour cream

½ lb. meat flanken
bones (any kind)
2 or 3 table spoons sugar
2 lemons
white vinegar
salt
1 clove garlic

Cook meat with little water for ½ hour in seperate pot. Prepare beats as above, add meat, bones, water and onion and cook till meat is done. Add 2 or 3 table spoons sugar, 1 teaspoon salt, lemon juice and dash of vinegar. Taste... Crush garlic with salt and pepper, disolve in bit of cold water, add garlic after light has been turned down.

FROM CANNED BEET (cubed, whole, or sliced)

Add one can of water to one can of beets, little sugar salt, white vinegar, (or lemon) grate an onion. Boil for a minute or two, taste. When cool add a measure of sour cream.

Sprin

10 young potatoes
1 parsely root and greens
1 piece of celery
1 onion
2 carrots
½ package noodles
1 tsp. salt
1 tabsp. butter

soup

Cut potatoes into cubes. Add parseley root, celery, (cut up) onion (whole), one quart of water, boil till potatoes are done, add another pint of water (boiling) let soup come to a boil. Add ½ tablespoon of butter and the noodles and boil eight more minutes✱ Add 1 teaspoon salt.
When serving add chopped parseley and a small piece of butter to every portion.

✱ Add boiling water if soup is too thick
Take soup greens out before serving

SPLIT PEA or

ONE CUP OF SPLIT PEAS

ONE ONION

ONE PARSELY ROOT

ONE CARROT

TWO PIECES OF CELERY

CLOVE OF GARLIC

42

LENTIL SOUP

TWO FRANKFURTERS

ONE TEASPOON SALT

FOUR TEASPOONS OF BUTTER

WASH THE PEAS WELL. COOK PEAS, ONION, CELERY, CARROT IN FOUR CUPS OF WATER, IN A COVERED POT, WITH A SMALL FLAME, AND LET BOIL FOR AN HOUR OR HOUR AND A HAL

ADD BUTTER AND SALT DURING COOKING. if soup gets too thick during cooking add a cup of boiling water. Remove all vegetables when soup is cooked

WHEN READY FOR SERVING... MASH GARLIC WITH SALT AND PEPPER, DIL- UTE WITH A LITTLE COLD WATER AND MIX INTO SOUP. WASH FRANKFURTERS CUT INTO SMALL PIECES AND LET SOUP BOIL FOR A MINUTE OR TWO.

VARIATIONS

serve toasted, fried in butter bread cubes, instead of frankfurters. serve with chopped parsley greens instead of garlic Use marrow bones or breast bones instead of butter, but cook those in the soup from the beginning.

VEGETABLE SOUP

1 lb. of mixed vegetables
- 1 onion
- 1 potatoe
- 1/8 cowliflower
- 1/2 parsnip
- 1/2 parsely root
- 1/4 celery
- 1 carrot
- stringbeans
- peas
- limabeans

1 tablespoon of barley
1/4 lb. of mushrooms
salt
1 1/2 tablespoons of butter ⁀ or bones
- BREAST BONES
- MARROW "
- VEAL "
- 1/4 CHICKEN

44

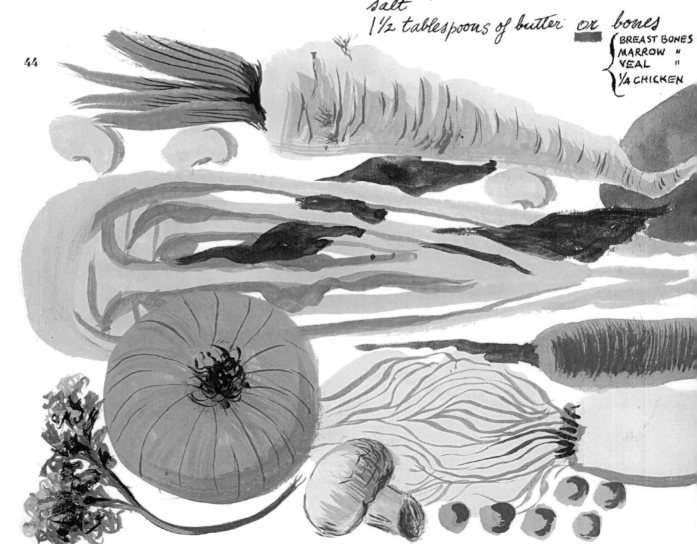

Clean and cut up all vegetables (except onion, parsnip, parsely root)
Rinse barley, and cook with vegetables in quart (or more) of
water till vegetables are all done. (two hours about.)
During last half hour of cooking add sliced mushrooms and
cubed potatoe and butter.* Add hot water during cooking
whenever necessary. Salt to taste, when you add the mushrooms
Remove whole onion, parsely root and parsnip when done.

* when you cook with bones, cook those from the very beginning

45

Cabbage Soup

WITH SOUR CREAM

1 head of cabbage, 2 lb.
1 teasp. salt
1 tabsp. sugar
1½ lemon
1 tabsp. flower
1 glass milk
4 medium onions
1 pint sour cream

Shred cabbage into pot, add salt, sugar; pour 1½ quarts boiling water into pot and let boil (with cover on) for ¾ hour.   Add juice of lemons. Mix flour smooth with the milk, add to cabbage and let it boil for another 5 minutes. Fry onions in butter. When cool mix with sour cream, and add to cooling soup. Serve at room temperature with parsley potatoes.

WITH MEAT

1 cabbage
1 med. can tomatoe
½ lb. soupmeat (flanken) with flatbone
2 marrow bones
1 large onion
½ tablesp. salt
3 tablesp. sugar
4 tablsp. honey
3 tablsp. vinegar
1 tablsp. flour

Shred cabbage into pot. Add strained tomatoes, meat, bones, diced onion, salt, sugar, 2 pints of water and let it cook till meat is done: (about 1½ hours) Stir honey in pan, over small flame, till brownish, add a bit of vinegar at a time, mixing all the time, till it comes to a boil, and pour over cabbage.   If cabbage is too thin, smoothe 1 tablespoon of flour into paste with cold water. Add more water gradually till it's a smooth liquid.   Add this mixture to cabbage and let boil for another five minutes.

Lima bean soup

½ lb. lima beans
or 1 lb. young limas
¼ lb. mushrooms
¾ cup shells →
soup greens
    ½ knap celery
    1 parsely root
    1 carrot
    2 pieces celery
    ½ parsnip
    1 leek

1 onion
salt

CARUS
BRAND

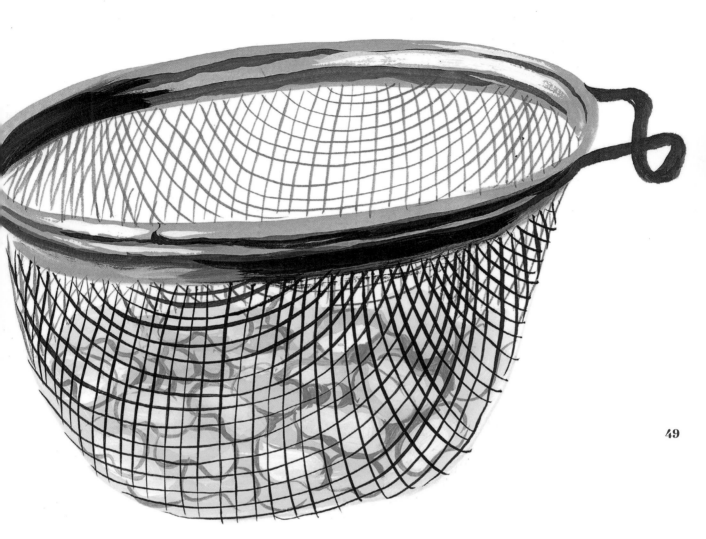

Boil soup greens and lima beans in quart
(or a little more) of water till limas are done.
(about 3/4 hour). (If too much soup boils out in
cooking, replace with boiling water)
Remove soup greens, except carrot, which gets
cut up and put back in the soup.

Just before serving add sliced mushrooms, salt to
taste, and the shells. Boil for another 8 to 10 minutes.
Fry crisp finely chopped onion, in butter and mix
with soup.

Potatoe

CELERY
ROOT PARSELY
CARROT
ONION
4 POTATOES
TABLESPOON BUTTER
2 TABLESPOONS FLOUR
DASH OF PARIKA
SALT
TEASPOON OF KASHA
PARSELY GREENS

- Boil whole soup green vegetables in pint of water, in covered pot over small flame for 3/4 of an hour.

- Melt butter, add flour and paprika, mix all the time until it is light brown. (5 MIN.) Add to this mixture 1 glass cold water mixing all the time, till it comes to a boil.

- Remove soup greens from soup. Add above mixture to soup. Add cubed potatoes. Add pint of boiling water, kasha and salt to taste. Cook till potatoes are done. (15 MIN) Serve with finely chopped parsely in each plate.

Soup

Karaway seed soup with dumplings

2 tablesp. seeds
1 tablesp. butter
2 tablesp. flour
salt

Wash seeds very well and cook in quart of water in covered pot. Let Boil for five minutes. Strain through fine sieve. Throw out seeds. Melt butter in frying pan (small) add flour, stirr constantly till light brown. (5 min.) Add half glass of cold water stirring all the time, add half cup soup, keep stirring, till mixture comes to a boil and is perfectly smooth.
Mix into soup, salt to taste and boil for five minutes.

DUMPLINGS

1 egg
1½ tablesp. flour
1 tablesp. milk
pinch of salt

beat the egg. Add salt, flour and milk, mix till very smooth. With wet clean spoon take small portions of dough and immerse into boiling soup each time. Let boil with dumplings 5 more minutes

54

Goulash

2 lb. MIDDLE CHUCK or SIRLOIN STEAK *cut up by butcher*
4 LARGE ONIONS
1 TEASPOON SALT
PAPRICA
1 CLOVE GARLIC
1 TOMATOE*
½ GREEN PEPPER
1 LARGE POTATOE
½ TEASPOON KARAWAY SEEDS
FLOUR

Cut into chunks onion, tomatoe, green pepper. Add
salt and paprica and simmer for a few minutes in
a heavy aluminum pan.
Wash meat, sprinkle with flour and paprica and add
to the above.   cover and let stew, on small light till
meat is almost tender.* (Stirr from time to time)
Add cubed potatoes, carraway seeds, stirr thoroughly
and stew for another half hour.
Add boiling water during cooking, if necessary

* about one hour and a half.
* one carrot, optional

55

4 SHOULDER OR RIB

56

FLOUR

SALT

1 EGG

CRISC
1 tablesp.

BREADCRUMBS

VEAL

CHOPS *(first cut)* CUTLETS

Salt and pepper chops, sprinkle with flour, dip into egg, (which has been mixed with salt) dip into crumbs.

Place cutlets into pan with very hot crisco and butter.
Fry on one side (on pretty brisk flame) till golden brown. Turn over chops, make a small flame, cover pan, and let cook slowly till meat is soft. (20 to 30 minutes) (Or put into oven with cover on).
Before serving uncover chops, and leave them on small flame, till they get crisp (10 minutes)

57

PEPPER

BUTTER

Brisket of Beef

2 lb. first cut breast of beef ✳
1 large onion, *sliced*
1 clove of garlic
1 tomatoe
paprica
salt
flour

If meat is very fresh, salt it, wrap in wax paper and
keep in frigidaire overnight or longer.
Simmer onion, garlic and tomatoe for a few minutes, in heavy pan.
Wash meat, salt and paprica it, put into pan above, on slow flame,
cover, and cook, allowing one hour to every pound of meat.
Turn meat over from time to time till meat is brown and
tender. Add a little boiling water whenever necessary.

When cooked take the meat out on a platter,
and let it get cold.
Add a little flour to the gravy and mix well
with fork, till onions are smooth.
Slice cold meat into ½ inch slices.
Add to the gravy and reheat in the
oven for about 20 minutes. Baste once.

✳ Have butcher trim off part of
the fat.

ROAST CHICKEN or DUCK or GOOSE

Filling for necks.
2 tblsp. beef breast fat
4 tblsp. flour
1 tsp. farina
salt, pepper, paprica

Work as for pie crust
adding fat to flour
and mixing with pastry
knife or fingers. Add
remaining ingredients.
Sew one end of neck. Fill a
little more than 2/3 full. Sew other end
wash with cold water. Pour boiling water over neck and pluck off any feathers
that remain. Roast with chicken. . . When stuffing birds, use ra
about 1/3 cup of fat to 1 cup of flour. (You will need 1 lb of fat). Do not quite
fill birds, as stuffing swells.

CHICKEN *freshkilled*
LARGE ONION
2 CLOVES GARLIC
SALT
PAPRICA
½ GLASS WATER

Clean chicken in cold water, inside and outside. Pour boiling water over it, and scrape skin. Wash again in cold water. Wash gizzard as directed in "CHICKEN SOUP". Salt inside and outside and score in refrigerator over night

Cut onion and garlic, into roasting pan, add water and bring to a boil. Put chicken in breast side down, sprinkle with paprica, cover and cook on top of range, on medium light. Turn on each side, till tender and add boiling water when necessary.

Brown in hot oven for 15 minutes, turning it over, till its nice and brown all over. If necessary add more water.

After chicken is finished, strain gravy. Cut chicken when cold into serving portions. Reheat in hot oven with gravy poured over top of chicken. Baste frequently and add water to gravy when necessary.

NOTE if chicken is fat, remove fat, cut into small pieces and cook till clear. Put up in glass jar and store in frigidaire.

Fry livers seperately in a little chicken fat

FOLLOW same procedure when you cook chicken inside of stove. Do not remove cover, till ready to brown.

DUCK follow same procedure as above. Rub duck with garlic

GOOSE, follow same procedure but cook inside of stove. Rub with garlic. If goose is fat no water is added during cooking.

Fat is drained off from time to time. Goose cooks with breast side up. Below longer time for browning. Goose fat, drained off is boiled till clear.

61

STUF
PEPF

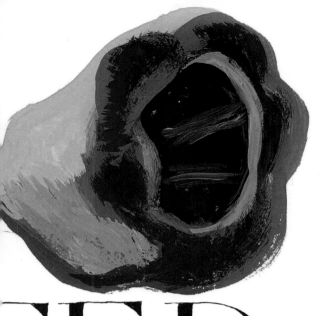

FFED
ERS

12 Green peppers
1½ lb ground meat
½ cup half cooked rice
1 large onion
1 tablesp. chicken fat
1 egg
salt
pepper
1 lb canned tomatoes
1 tablesp. sugar
1 teasp. salt
12 gingersnaps

Wash peppers, cut out hole where stem is, take out all seeds and fibres inside.

Grate onion into meat, add salt pepper, egg, chickenfat, rice, and mix. Stuff peppers with this mixture and replace stem.

Place peppers, stem side up into roasting pan. Put tomatoes through sieve, pour over peppers. Sprinkle with sugar and salt, cover, and allow to simmer on small light for one hour.

Cover snaps with cold water. When disolved, mix thoroughly, add to peppers and simmer for 15 minutes.

Lamb stew

2 lb shoulder of lamb cut into small
    pieces, fat cut away
4 large onions
1 tablsp. salt
paprica
1 clove of garlic
1 tomatoe
1 bunch of carrots
½ lb. lima beans
1 large diced potatoe
½ lb. peas

Cut up onions, tomatoe, garlic,
into heavy large pan, add paprika
and simmer with cover on for
a few minutes.

Wash meat thoroughly and
without draining place on top
of onions. (This will be all the
water needed) Sprinkle meat
with salt, flour and paprica.
Add carrots cut in disks, and
lima beans. Cover and allow
to simmer gently for about
an hour. Stirr from time to time

Add peas and potatoes, stirr
thoroughly and stew on a
low flame for about ½ hour.

P.S. add hot water during
cooking if absolutely necessary.

serve wit

IKALACHA
meat balls cooked like fish

2 lb of lean steak, ground
or 1 lb shoulder of veal
1 lb top round of beef

6 large onions
1½ glasses of water
2 teasp. sugar
2 heaping teasp. salt
pepper

Cut into rings four onions.
Add the water, one teasp
sugar, one heaping teasp
salt and boil in fairly
large pan for 15 minutes

Grate into the meat two
onions. Mix well with the
remaining sugar and salt
and some fresh ground pepper.
Roll into small meat balls
and add them to the boiling
onions. Cover and cook for
about 3/4 hour.

Turn off heat, sprinkle
generously with fresh ground
pepper, and cover pan for 5 more
minutes. Take out meat balls, mash
onions with fork, and replace meat.

Heat before serving, or serve
cold with plenty of bread for
dunking.

67

very fresh crusty bread...DUNKSTYLE

68

KALACHA
meatloaf

2 lb top round, ground
2 eggs
2 onions
2 tomatoes
1½ tablesp. breadcrumbs
1 tablesp. chickenfat
½ green pepper
1 clove garlic
salt
pepper
paprica

Cut up one onion, one tomatoe, garlic, green pepper. Add a little chicken fat, and let simmer with cover on.
Grind the other onion and tomatoe into the meat; add chicken fat, eggs, salt, pepper, breadcrumbs, and 2 tablespoons of cold water. Mix well.
Shape into meatloaf (or into individual small loaves). Place into pan with simmering onions. Sprinkle generously with paprica, cover and cook on each side ¾ of an hour — or put into the oven after the first ¾ hour. (without the cover) Baste once or twice.

Schnitzel

2 lb of ground top round
1 onion
1 tomato
1 tablesp. breadcrumbs
1 tablesp. chickenfat
2 eggs
3 tablesp. spry
2 teasp. salt
breadcrumbs for dipping

Grind the onion and tomatoe into meat. Add the breddcrumbs chicken fat, eggs, salt and mix well. Shape into flat round cakes, dip into bread crumbs, and make a criss cross pattern with knife. Turn on other side and repeat.

Melt one heaping tablesp. of spry in large frying pan. When spry is very hot, place meat patties into pan. Allow to brown on one side (about 8 minutes) and turn. Fry on other side. Add more spry during cooking. Serve with German fried potatoes.

ROAST VEAL
with stuffing

BREAST OF VEAL
4½ lb equals 6 portions
butcher to make pocket
LARGE ONION
2 CLOVES GARLIC
TABLESP. CHICKEN FAT
SALT , PAPRICA

STUFFING {
onion
tablesp. chicken fat
3 eggs
tablesp. chopped parsley
2 tablesp. chopped celery hearts
2 hard rolls
salt , pepper
}

Cut one onion very fine. Fry till golden brown and crisp in spoonfull of chicken fat, stirring all the time.
Beat the eggs well with some salt and pepper. Add parsely and celery.
Soak two small rolls (without crust) in cold water for 5 minutes. Squeese out water and mix with the eggs etc.
Add fried onions, mix again and stuff the veal pocket. Sew up pocket.

Rub salt into veal with garlic. Sprinkle with paprica.
Cut onion into quarters. Add the garlic and chicken fat and simmer in roasting pan for few minutes.
Put veal into pan, boneside up.
Place covered into hot oven.
Add water and baste whenever needed
Turn over after one hour
Cook for another hour.

Let cool. When cold slice into six portions and reheat in hot oven, for about 15 minutes, basting once or twice.

74

Fricassee

goose or chicken giblets (neck, wings, gizzard, liver*)
   2 medium size onions , 1 clove garlic
1 teasp. chicken fat (goose giblets need no fat)
salt(½ teasp.) paprica , pepper , flour (½ teasp.)
   ½ cup water   { small onion
                                                    { ½ egg
½ lb. ground steak , prepared like schnitzel   { salt, pepper
                                                    { chickenfat

Cut onions and garlic into heavy pan. Add fat, salt and paprica
and allow to stew for a little while. Cut neck into four pieces;
also cut up gizzard, wings and add to the pan. Add water, cover
and cook on small light for an hour.
Roll chopped meat into small balls and add to giblets. Add
a little hot water if necessary and cook for another 20 minutes.
Sprinkle with flour about 10 minutes before serving, mix well.
Hot water may be added from time to time during cooking,
if necessary. There should not be too much gravy
* liver should be added about 10 minutes before fricassee is done and
after flour has been added.

Stuffe

Cabbage

1 CABBAGE
1½ lb ground steak
½ cup half cooked rice
3 onions
1 tablesp. chicken fat
1 egg
2 teasp. salt
2 tablesp. sugar
1 medium can tomato sauce
4 tablesp. honey
1 lemon
8 gingersnaps

Put cabbage into pot of boiling water, allow to boil with cover on, for one minute, and leave in water for about five minutes. Seperate from cabbage 18 leaves, and shave stems if they are thick.

Grate into meat one onion. Add salt,* sugar,* pepper, egg, chicken fat and rice. Mix well and place a generous tablespoon of this mixture inside each cabbage leaf.

Fold over one side of cabbage leaf over meat. Begin rolling leaf from stem part down. Tuck in open side, like a package. Roll up all eighteen leaves.

Remainder of cabbage shred into pot. Slice one onion into pot. Add tablespoon of sugar, and teaspoon of salt. Place cabbage rolls tightly in one layer. Slice the other onion over this layer. Put in second layer of cabbage rolls. Pour over this tomato sauce, cover and cook on small light 1½ hours.

Stir honey in pan over small light till slightly brownish and pour into cabbage. Add the juice of one lemon. Add gingersnaps, which have been disolved in a bit of cold water. Let the whole thing boil for 10 or 15 minutes.

* one teaspoon
* one tablespoon

77

POTTED LIVER

Slice four or five onion into pan and brown with cover on in a tablespoon of chicken fat. Add three sliced mushrooms cover and bring to a boil. Add a small amount of hot water.

Heat frying pan until very hot. Sear (1 lb) slices of calves liver, allowing to remain in pan about one minute on each side. Cut in strips, dredge with flour and paprika and add to the onions and mushrooms. Add a teaspoon of salt and allow to boil for 5 or six minutes.

with hardboiled eggs

Add two sliced hardboiled eggs and some freshly ground pepper just before serving.

1 lb. liver
4 onions
1 tablesp. chicken fat
3 mushrooms
1 tablesp. flour
1 teasp. salt
2 eggs
pepper

WILD RICE

Wash rice in several waters.
Drain.
Add a little at a time to rapidly boiling water (salted), boil till tender, 25 to 35 minutes.
Drain, rinse, (with very hot water) cover with towel & place collander over boiling water *to fluff.*
80 *(about 20 minutes)*

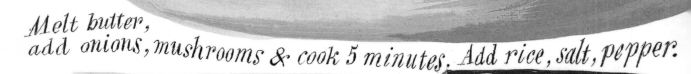

Melt butter, add onions, mushrooms & cook 5 minutes. Add rice, salt, pepper.

Stir & heat thoroughly.

1 cup rice
2 quts. water
3 tbsp. salt
1/4 cup butter
1 onion,
(chopped fine)
1 cup mushrooms
(sliced thin)
salt & pepper

K

asha (Buckwheat) GROATS

1 cup groats
1 egg
1 teaspoon salt
2 cups boiling water
1 tablespoon butter

Put groats in heavy skillet.
Stir in egg and keep stirring over medium flame till grains become aromatic.
Add boiling water, (the mixture will sputter and splash for seconds) reduce heat to minimum, stir in butter & salt, cover. Cook for 25 minutes.
Serve hot with meat, **or** with milk, cream and sugar for breakfast

BULBENICK BAKE

¾ c. FLOUR
1 YEAST CAKE
4 LARGE POTATOES
2 t. FARINA
1 T. BUTTER
SALT
PEPPER

Sift flour into large bowl and make a well in the center.

Crumple and disolve yeast in a quarter cup lukewarm water and pour into well.

Mix it with some of the flour into thick paste and put bowl in warm place.

Grate well scrubbed potatoes, s

POTATO PAN CAKE

and all. Drain off liquid. Combine grated potatoes with flour and yeast mixture. Season with salt and pepper. Stirr in, farina and allow to rise in a warm place for about 1½ hours.

Pour well stirred mixture into a generously buttered 10" X 15" shallow pan. Bake in very hot oven for ¾ hour. Turn, and brown other side for 15 minutes. Cut in pan and serve hot with meats.

VARIATION

Grate potatoes and drain off liquid. Add two eggs, salt, pepper and one tablespoon of bread crumbs.

Heat a tablespoon of oil in pan till very hot. Pour in mixture and bake in very hot oven for about one hour. 85

CIPE'S RECIPES REVISITED

SARAH RICH

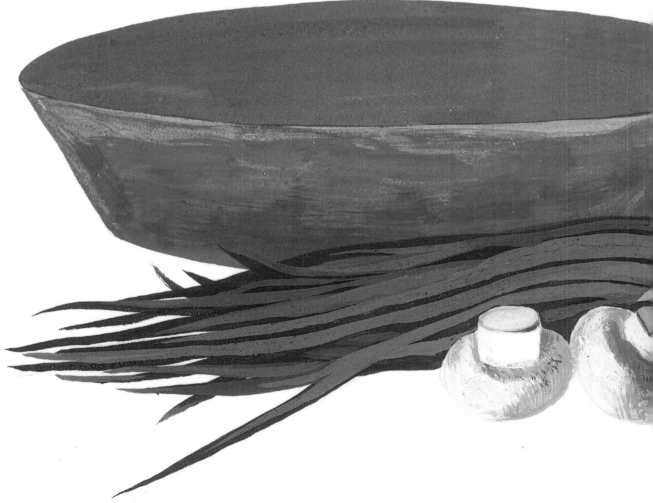

In the following pages, I have approached the recipes in Cipe's paintings as a historic preservationist—that is, I've attempted to repair what may be broken, update what's no longer feasible or appropriate to our culinary moment, yet at the same time preserve the intention and integrity of the original dish. These recipes were handed (or more likely, recited) to Cipe by her mother, and they were all so familiar to Jewish immigrants of that time that it wouldn't have been necessary to mention every step in the process. Things were taken as given, and a basic knowledge of the cuisine was assumed. So here I have attempted to remove some of those assumptions and make the instructions clearer, and the ingredients perhaps a bit more accessible to the modern cook and enticing to the modern eater.

CHICKEN SOUP

*U*ntil trying Cipe's version of chicken soup, I'd never heard of using beef bones to enrich a chicken broth.

But now I may never do it any other way. Her recipe calls for flanken, which is more commonly found as short rib at today's butcher counters, unless you go to a kosher butcher. Of course, kosher meat has been brined, so if you're not using kosher meat, this recipe calls for salting the chicken and beef a day ahead to get the same effect. In Cipe's original recipe, much of her instruction revolves around preparing the chicken, which in the 1940s would have been purchased with feathers and organs still in the bird. We get to skip all those steps, which makes this a very simple recipe.

88

1 3- or 4-lb chicken (if not kosher, follow instructions for pre-salting)
1 lb beef short rib
1 yellow onion
1 celery stalk
1 parsnip
1 leek
3 carrots
½ lb frozen or fresh green peas
2 tbsp fresh dill, parsley, or a combination
Optional: egg noodles, matzo balls, or rice

If your meat is not kosher, do this first step 1 day ahead. Rinse and pat dry the chicken (removing livers, gizzards, or other parts that may come stuffed inside). Using about 1 tablespoon of kosher salt per pound, generously salt the chicken all over. Do the same with the short rib. Cover and refrigerate overnight. The following day it can be placed as is into the soup pot, no need to rinse.

To prepare the soup, place the chicken, short rib, onion, celery, parsnip, leek, and two carrots into a large stock pot. The vegetables do not need to be chopped. Fill with cold water to cover ingredients, plus an inch or two. Bring the pot to a boil and then turn to a simmer and allow to cook for at least 2 hours. It won't hurt the broth to cook it longer (up to 4 hours), but be sure the water doesn't evaporate so much that it exposes the bones and vegetables.

When the broth is done, strain out the liquid. Taste it and add salt if needed. Remember that the meat will have some saltiness too. From the strainer, pull out the chicken and set aside for returning to the soup. You can also reserve the beef to add back in, or use it for something else. The meat can be pulled or cubed according to preference.

When ready to serve, bring the broth back up to a low boil, add the frozen or fresh peas, and cook until tender. If including noodles or matzo balls, cook them first in a separate pot of salted water to avoid adding starch to the broth. Add the meat back into the pot, and shaved-thin slices of the final carrot. Turn off the heat and add in the fresh, roughly chopped herbs.

89

BORSCHT

lthough Cipe did not keep kosher, her recipes are a reflection of the way her mother cooked, which would have honored the tradition of keeping milk and meat separate.

For that reason, her borscht page features alternate variations on the classic beet soup. One contains sour cream and is meant to be eaten cold, while the other contains beef and is served hot. This update focuses on the cold, vegetarian soup.

4½ lbs beets (you can use red or golden; both make a soup that is incredibly vibrant)

1 yellow onion

3 cups vegetable or chicken stock (recipes on pages 124 and 125)

1 tsp sugar

2 tsp salt, plus more to taste

juice of 1 lemon

1–2 tbsp red wine vinegar

½ cup whole-milk yogurt

1 cup sour cream, divided (half will be used for serving)

1 bunch fresh dill

Rinse beets and place in a large pot. Slice the onion in half, leaving the skin on, and cover both with cold water by several inches. Bring to a boil, then simmer until beets are tender, about 30–40 minutes depending on the size of the beets. When done, drain and cool, then slip the skins off the beets (it is helpful to hold them under cool running water to do this).

Set aside one or two beets and cut the rest in halves or quarters, then throw into a food processor with the stock, sugar, salt, lemon juice, vinegar, yogurt, and ½ cup of the sour cream. Blend until smooth, adjusting thickness by adding more stock if needed. When smooth, taste and add more salt, lemon, or vinegar as needed to achieve desired brightness.

To serve, dice into small cubes the beets that were set aside. Ladle pureed borscht into a bowl, top with a generous helping of diced beets, a tablespoon of sour cream, and a hearty pinch of fresh dill.

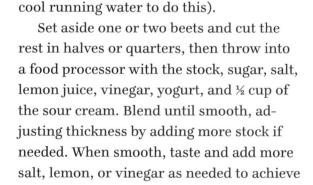

SPRING SOUP

In Cipe's original recipe for this soup, she includes both potatoes and noodles and calls for removing the vegetables, which serve as flavoring agents in the cooking process, before serving.

As a result, all the colors that features so beautifully in the painting of the recipe are lost in the bowl (she even painted a brilliant green pea pod, but the recipe doesn't call for peas, so we've added them). The update uses vegetable stock made ahead so that the vegetables in the soup itself cook for a shorter time, retain their flavor, and are meant to be eaten. Since the soup is called "spring," this version takes a cue from the French *soupe au pistou*, adding a scoop of herby pesto at the end. The result is an edible version of Cipe's painting.

2 carrots

2 celery stalks

1 large leek, rinsed

1 shallot

1 zucchini or yellow squash

1 lb (about 12) potatoes (Yukon gold or red new potatoes work well)

6 cups vegetable or chicken stock

8 oz fresh or frozen green peas

1 cup small pasta, ditalini or mini shells

1 bunch fresh basil

2 tbsp olive oil

Optional: 2 tbsp grated parmesan and a parmesan rind for flavoring the soup

Chop carrot and celery into small chunks and slice leek (white portion) and shallot thinly. In a deep pot, heat 2 tablespoons of olive oil over medium heat and add the chopped vegetables, sautéing until they soften but do not brown.

Wash and cube the potatoes, halve and slice zucchini or squash, and add to the pot with the other vegetables. Give a few stirs, season with a generous pinch of salt (if your stock is salted, you will need less salt here), then add vegetable stock. If the stock does not cover the vegetables, add water until everything is submerged by 2–3 inches. Bring to a boil, then turn to simmer and cook for 15 minutes, until the potatoes begin to get tender. If using parmesan rind, add now and remove when the soup is done cooking.

While soup is cooking, boil a small pot of water and cook the pasta according to directions until al dente. Before the potatoes are completely soft, add peas and continue cooking until the pasta is done. When pasta is done, drain and add to soup pot. The pasta and potatoes should both be tender at this point, and the pot can be taken off the heat.

To finish the dish, wash basil and place in a small food processor or mortar and pestle. Drizzle in some oil and blend or mash into a paste, adding some kosher salt to help break down the basil leaves. If using parmesan, mix into basil paste at this point.

To serve the soup, ladle into bowls and top with a dollop of pesto. Leftover soup will thicken due to the pasta continuing to absorb some of the liquid. You can always add a bit of water or stock when reheating leftovers, though some people love the stewy quality of the day-old soup.

LENTIL SOUP

This is one of the few recipes in Cipe's collection that has the mark of mid-century American cooking, rather than the pure Old World European style of most of the others.

She uses beef hot dogs cut up in the soup—an economical and quick way to add flavor and meatiness to an otherwise mild legume soup. This update sticks with lentils, which hold up a bit better than split peas; uses sausage in place of the frankfurters; and includes vegetables in the final dish.

1 yellow onion
2 tbsp olive oil
1 clove garlic
2 carrots
1 celery stalk
1–2 Italian sausage links
   or beef hot dogs
1 cup dried lentils (brown
   or beluga)
4 cups vegetable stock (recipe
   on page 124)
2–4 cups water
2 cups chopped dark greens
   (kale, chard, spinach, or
   a combination)

Dice onion, finely slice garlic, and chop carrots into small rounds. Heat 2 tablespoons of olive oil in a soup pot. Add onion and stir until it begins to soften, then add carrot, garlic, and sausage. Cook for a few minutes until the meat is gently browning, then add lentils, stock, and water. If using unsalted stock, add a pinch of salt now, but not the full amount you'll want for the final dish. You can season further at the end. Bring to a boil, then simmer until the lentils are tender, about 20–25 minutes. At the end, add the chopped greens and allow to wilt in the soup. Add additional salt to taste.

93

VEGETABLE SOUP

*S*everal of Cipé's recipes are, essentially, vegetable soups.

One is a "Spring Soup," (recipe on page 91), but this vegetable soup recipe produces a heartier, more wintry dish, with barley and mushrooms giving it weight and body. Chicken or beef stock can be used in place of vegetable.

2–3 dried porcini mushrooms
1 tbsp olive oil
1 tbsp butter
1 yellow onion, diced
1 parsnip, chopped
1 carrot, chopped
1 celery stalk, chopped
1 cup sliced cremini mushrooms
½ cup barley
8 cups stock, water, or a combination
1 cup green beans, halved
1 cup fresh or frozen peas

94

Place dried porcinis in a cup or small bowl of hot water to soften. Meanwhile, heat a tablespoon of olive oil and a tablespoon of butter in a soup pot. Add diced onion and cook for a minute or two to soften, then add chopped parsnip, carrot, and celery. Stir until fragrant. Remove porcinis from water (reserve the soak water!) and chop small. Add cremini and porcini mushrooms to the pot, season with a generous sprinkle of salt, and cook until the mushrooms start to release some of their water. Then add barley to the pot and cover with porcini soaking water and stock. Bring to a boil, then simmer until the barley has begun to expand, about 20 minutes. At this point, add 1–2 teaspoons of salt, the green beans, and the peas. Continue cooking until barley is done. Taste and add salt if needed.

CABBAGE SOUP

As with the borscht recipe, Cipe's cabbage recipe is written in two versions—one with dairy and the other with meat—to respect kosher rules.

This is a meat version of the cabbage soup. With its use of flanken (short rib), tomato, and the acid touch of vinegar, this recipe begs to be treated more like a stew than a soup. In her original, the cabbage steeps in the soup for the duration of the cooking time, making quite a pungent concoction; in the update, the meat is browned and cooked with tomato and aromatics first, adding the cabbage near the end. By adding honey, Cipe makes the final flavor sweet and sour. Here it's toned down a bit, but included as a nod to her intention.

3 tbsp olive or other neutral,
  high-heat oil
1 lb short rib, bone on,
  cut into four pieces by
  the butcher
1 onion
1 celery stalk
2 carrots
1 beef marrow bone
1 28-oz can chopped
  tomatoes
2–4 cups vegetable
  or beef stock
1 head cabbage
1 tbsp honey
1–2 tbsp red wine vinegar
1 tbsp all-purpose flour
  (optional)

Heat oil in a heavy bottom pot, add short rib, and brown on all sides. Allow this process to happen slowly, not disturbing the meat as it browns, so that it doesn't stick to the pan. After several minutes cooking on each side, add the onion, celery, and carrot, all chopped small; drop in the marrow bone, and cover with the whole can of tomatoes and at least 2 cups of stock. Cook the soup for 1 hour, checking the meat for doneness. When the meat is tender and falling off the bone, pull it out, remove it from the bones, and chop it to the desired serving size.

Keeping the meat set aside, core the cabbage and chop it into thin strips. Add it to the hot soup and simmer until softened. Then add the meat back in and season the soup with the honey, and vinegar. Finally, if using, put flour into a small bowl and pour ¼ cup of the soup broth over it, stirring to a thin paste. Add the flour mixture back into the soup, stir, and cook 10–20 more minutes until the broth is thickened.

95

LIMA BEAN SOUP

This soup works with frozen lima beans, but starting with dried beans makes a tastier, more flavorful dish.

Again, using vegetable stock you've made ahead (recipe on page 124) makes this more efficient, although adding some flavorful vegetables and herbs to the bean cooking liquid prior to making the soup gives even more dimension. Cipe called for mushrooms, which would likely have been white button, but using dried wild mushrooms provides considerably more flavor and spares the sometimes-spongy texture of a floating white mushroom. Likewise, farro or barley brings nuttiness to the soup and prevents the mushy, starchy potential of a long-cooked pasta. The lima beans will become very soft and creamy with cooking. If you want a firmer bean, try great northern or cannellini.

½ lb dried lima beans
1 yellow onion
2 celery stalks
1 sprig thyme
1 bay leaf
1 shallot, chopped
1 handful or a store-bought pack of dried wild mushrooms (porcini, chanterelle, etc.)
1 tbsp olive oil
8 cups vegetable or chicken stock
¼ cup pearl farro or barley
1–2 tbsp fresh parsley and chives, chopped

Cover dried beans with water in a bowl or pot and soak overnight. The following day, drain and rinse the beans, then place in a soup pot and cover with fresh water. Add whole onion, celery stalk, thyme, and bay leaf, bring to a boil, then simmer until beans are just tender. Drain again and set aside. Meanwhile, soak dry mushrooms in a bowl of warm water.

Heat a tablespoon of olive oil in the soup pot and add shallot, allowing it to soften but not brown. Chop up rehydrated mushrooms and add them to the pot. Add beans back in and cover with stock. If stock is unsalted, add salt at this stage so that as the beans finish, they'll soak up some seasoning. Add farro or barley, bring to a boil, then turn down to a simmer and cook until grain is done, about 30 minutes. To serve, add chopped fresh herbs and a grind of fresh black pepper if desired. A little butter stirred in at the end doesn't hurt.

POTATO SOUP

A *potato soup should be simple, and Cipe's is. She begins by making a vegetable stock, then makes a roux, then mixes it all with cubed potatoes* and a tiny sprinkling of kasha (whole buckwheat). The end. Of course, with the modern advantages of blenders and food processors, we can take these basics to a smoother point by pureeing some or all of the soup, resulting in a creamy texture without the floury roux.

1 onion

3 leeks (white part and about an inch of green)

1 celery stalk

1 small celery root (or parsnip, if you prefer)

2 tbsp unsalted butter

4–5 russet potatoes, peeled and cubed

1 tsp kasha (optional)

8 cups vegetable or chicken stock

¼ tsp paprika

2 tbsp chopped Italian parsley

Chop onion, leeks, celery, and celery root, making sure to slice off all the tough exterior of the celery root. Melt the butter in a large soup pot and add chopped vegetables, stirring until they soften but do not brown. Add potatoes, kasha if using, and stock, supplementing with water if the vegetables aren't completely covered. Season liquid with 2–3 teaspoons of salt, bring to a boil, then turn down to a simmer until potatoes become tender.

Once potatoes are tender, turn off the heat and allow to cool slightly. Scoop one cup of the soup into a blender or food processor and puree until smooth (using caution, as hot liquids in these machines tend to burst out if the container is too full). Add the puree back to the soup pot, stir in chopped parsley, sprinkle with paprika, and serve. This soup can also be pureed in its entirety, one cup at a time, and will result in a silky, smooth soup.

97

CARAWAY SOUP
WITH DUMPLINGS

Cipe's recipe for caraway soup with dumplings may make you wonder what kind of strange dish it will yield.

The broth consists only of caraway-steeped water—essentially a tea—combined with a flour-and-butter roux, finished with spoonfuls of dumpling dough. It's a traditional Hungarian dish called *Köménymagleves*, and, like the painting Cipe created to accompany the recipe, it doesn't have a lot of color or detail. To modernize things a bit, this updated recipe leans toward a more classic chicken soup infused with caraway, creating a flavorful broth by poaching chicken breasts in the cooking water and adding caraway to the dumplings themselves.

98

1 tbsp oil

½ large yellow onion, chopped

1–2 carrots, chopped

1 celery stalk, chopped

1 split chicken breast (two halves) with skin on and bone in

½ tbsp whole caraway seeds

¾ cup milk

2 tbsp unsalted butter

½ cup all-purpose flour

¼ cup rye flour

1 egg

¼ tsp whole caraway seeds, ground in mortar and pestle, or pre-ground caraway

¼ tsp salt, plus more for seasoning the cooking liquid

In a large soup pot, heat oil, then add onion, carrot, and celery and stir until softened but not brown. Add chicken breasts and whole caraway seeds, and fill pot with 8 cups cold water. Season water generously with salt (at least 2 teaspoons). Bring to a boil, then turn to a low simmer. Some foam will form on the surface, which can be skimmed and discarded. Allow chicken to cook completely, about 40 minutes. Check for doneness and continue cooking until the meat is cooked through. When done, remove chicken from soup and set aside to cool.

While the soup is cooling, make dumpling batter. Lightly beat the egg in a small bowl. Heat milk and butter in a small pot until just below a simmer. Add flours, salt, and ground seeds into the milk mixture and continue stirring a minute or so until it thickens. Remove from heat and allow to cool slightly. Add a generous spoonful of the soup broth to the egg and whisk quickly to warm the egg a bit and prevent it from cooking upon hitting the pot. Then pour the egg mixture into the flour and milk mixture, stirring to incorporate the egg without cooking it. The dough should be slightly sticky.

Bring soup back to a low boil and drop dumpling dough by spoonfuls into the broth, allowing the dumplings to cook for 4–5 minutes. They will rise to the surface as they cook through, but let them go another minute after they float to reduce any gluey texture in the center.

When chicken is cool, discard skin and remove meat from bones. Shred or chop meat as desired and add back to the soup before serving.

99

GOULASH

*G*oulash sounds like a fabled dish from a fairy tale—something that would have been eaten in a forest by a witch or a wolf.

But in fact, it is a simple stew of beef and potatoes, slow-cooked and hearty. This recipe uses some chicken stock and additional aromatic vegetables to fill out the flavor, but otherwise stays true to tradition.

1½-lb whole boneless chuck roast

4 tsp kosher salt, divided

2 tbsp oil

2 medium carrots, diced

2 celery stalks, diced

2 cloves garlic, slivered

1 yellow onion, sliced thinly

1 red bell pepper, de-stemmed, seeded, and sliced thinly

5 early girl or plum tomatoes, cored and cut into small rough chunks (or 1 15-oz can of chopped tomatoes)

¼ cup ground sweet Hungarian paprika

3 cups chicken stock

1 bay leaf

1 tbsp all-purpose flour

1 cup fingerling or Yukon gold potatoes, peeled and cut into 1-inch cubes

Adjust oven rack to middle position and preheat to 350°.

Cut the chuck into three steaks, season all sides evenly with 2 teaspoons kosher salt, and set aside.

Heat oil in a large Dutch oven on medium-high and add the steaks. Sear on both sides until well browned, avoiding touching them so that they don't stick, about 4–5 minutes per side. Transfer the steaks to a plate. Reduce heat to medium-low. Add carrots and celery to Dutch oven and sear on all sides until dark golden brown, about 5 minutes. Reduce the heat if necessary to avoid scorching. Add yellow onion, red bell pepper, tomatoes, paprika, and 1 teaspoon salt to the Dutch oven. Stir until onions and peppers begin to soften and paprika becomes fragrant, about 2–3 minutes. Next add the chicken stock mixture, 1 teaspoon kosher salt, and bay leaf. Turn the heat back up and bring to a simmer.

Cut the steaks into 1-inch cubes, place in a bowl, and toss with flour to coat. Add the cubed beef to the Dutch oven, simmer for 1 minute, and transfer pot to the oven with a lid on, partially ajar. Cook for 1 hour or until beef starts to become tender. The liquid should be simmering throughout. At 1 hour, check meat for tenderness and add the potatoes to the pot and cook for 40 minutes more.

At 40 minutes, check potatoes for doneness. If they are tender, remove pot from the oven. Serve hot with toasted bread and freshly chopped parsley.

VEAL CUTLETS

In Cipe's original veal cutlet recipe, the meat is coated in breadcrumbs before frying, but because her veal schnitzel recipe also calls for breaded, fried veal, we updated this to leave the cutlet naked in cooking, then added a toasted breadcrumb salsa on top—a modern take that we think Cipe would have approved of.

6 ¼-inch veal cutlets (about 1–1½ lbs)

1 cup fresh breadcrumbs, untoasted (from about 5–6 oz baguette or country bread)

2 medium shallots, finely diced

4 tsp champagne vinegar

¼ tsp kosher salt

½ tsp freshly ground black pepper

2 tbsp capers, finely chopped

1 bunch parsley, finely chopped

zest of 1 lemon

½ cup plus 2 tbsp extra virgin olive oil, divided

Season the cutlets: On a flat platter or baking pan, sprinkle both sides lightly with salt. Wrap with plastic or seal in an airtight container and refrigerate overnight, ideally, or at least 1 hour before cooking.

Prepare and toast the breadcrumbs. Preheat oven to 300°. If the crust of the bread is very thick and hard, shave off the exterior with a knife. Tear the trimmed bread into small pieces and transfer to a food processor. Pulse the bread until it has completely broken down into small crumbs. Place in a small bowl, toss with 1 tablespoon olive oil to coat well, then spread crumbs on a parchment-lined baking sheet and place in the oven. Toast for 3 minutes, then use a metal spatula to mix and turn crumbs, then bake for another 2–3 minutes. Breadcrumbs should be golden brown when done. If they aren't brown after two rounds of stirring and toasting, repeat until browned.

To prepare the salsa, combine the diced shallot, champagne vinegar, kosher salt, and ground pepper in a bowl. Let sit for at least 5 minutes so shallot can absorb vinegar. Add the chopped capers, parsley, lemon zest, toasted breadcrumbs, and ½ cup of the olive oil. Mix well.

To cook the cutlets, heat the last tablespoon of olive oil in a large sauté pan over high heat. Place the cutlets in the pan and cook for about 2 minutes on each side until cooked through and lightly brown. To serve, top each cutlet with the breadcrumb salsa.

103

BRISKET OF BEEF

Brisket is a Jewish classic and, when done right, one of the most delicious ways to eat a piece of beef. This recipe hews close to Cipe's original, with the addition of caraway seeds, which she uses elsewhere in the book, and which stays true to the Eastern European flavor palette. Be sure to start this a day in advance to allow the seasoning to sink into the meat before it's cooked.

104

2½ lbs beef brisket
2 tsp kosher salt
1 tsp freshly ground black pepper
1 tsp freshly ground caraway seeds
2 qts beef or chicken stock
2 tbsp virgin olive oil
1 onion, chopped
2 carrots, sliced
1 celery stalk, sliced
1 tbsp tomato paste
¼ cup red wine or apple cider vinegar
1 sprig each of rosemary and thyme

One day in advance, season the brisket evenly with kosher salt, pepper, and ground caraway seeds. Place in an airtight container in refrigerator overnight.

When ready to cook, preheat oven to 325°.

Remove the brisket from the refrigerator, place on a large cutting board, and slice into two even pieces. Allow to come to room temperature for 15–20 minutes. In a medium-size pot, bring stock to a boil, then reduce to a simmer.

In a large Dutch oven, heat the olive oil on high. Sear brisket on both sides until well browned, about 4–5 minutes per side, working one at a time if necessary. Once browned, remove from pot and set on a plate. Add the onions, carrots, and celery into the hot pot. Stir gently for a couple of minutes, until the vegetables begin to soften. Add the tomato paste and stir to dissolve. Add the vinegar and, after it bubbles up, gently scrape the bottom of the pot with a wooden spoon to loosen the bits the vinegar released.

Return the meat to the pot and pour the simmering stock over everything. Throw in the herb sprigs. Place lid on top of the pot, slightly ajar. Transfer to middle rack of oven. After 1 hour, check the meat, turning the pieces over and braising for another 90 minutes or until very tender. Once done, place the Dutch oven on the stovetop to cool.

When cool, remove the brisket and slice it against the grain into ¼- to ½-inch thick slices. Return meat to the cooking liquid and reheat. To serve, place brisket slices on a plate and ladle some of the liquid and vegetables over the top.

ROAST DUCK

C ipé's recipe for roasted poultry is a veritable wall of tiny text, describing steps that remind us of what cooking involved seventy-five years ago.

The home cook would have bought a bird that still had pin feathers and organs, and their removal added considerable work. Happily, we can skip those steps. Her recipe provides instructions for either a chicken, duck, or goose, so we decided to create a roasted duck recipe here.

1 4½–5-lb duck with wings trimmed off and giblets, feet, and neck removed
2 tsp kosher salt
½ tsp freshly ground black pepper
zest and juice of 1 lemon, divided
1 tbsp unsalted butter
1 clove garlic, sliced in half
2 sprigs rosemary, de-stemmed and finely chopped
1 tbsp all-purpose flour
water
1 cup chicken stock
kosher salt and freshly ground pepper

Season the duck: In a small bowl, combine the salt, pepper, and lemon zest. Mix well. Apply the salt/pepper/zest mix to the legs, breasts, and underneath loose skin directly on meat. Place the seasoned duck breast side up on a grated cooling rack on top of a baking sheet and loosely wrap it in plastic. Refrigerate at least 2 hours and up to 2 days before roasting.

When ready to roast: Adjust oven rack to middle position and preheat to 350°.

Take the duck out of the refrigerator, unwrap from plastic, and allow to come to room temperature on the rack for around 15 minutes. Once tempered, place the duck in the oven. After 10 minutes, check to make sure the skin is not browning too quickly. If it is, reduce heat to 325°. Continue roasting for another 45 minutes, rotating the pan 180° halfway through, until the skin is golden brown. Remove from oven and let rest on the same cooling rack.

Transfer the bird to a large cutting board, reserving the roasting sheet with the pan drippings. While the bird rests, make the pan sauce. Bring a medium-sized sauce pot to medium heat. Add the drippings from the roast duck along with butter, garlic, and rosemary. Whisk to combine. In a small bowl, place the flour and then slowly add ¼ cup of water, whisking constantly to create a smooth slurry. Add the slurry to the sauce pot and mix well. Simmer for 2 minutes and then add the chicken stock and juice from half of the lemon. Simmer for about 5–7 more minutes or until the sauce has thickened enough to coat a spoon and has reduced to about ¾ volume. Season to taste with salt and freshly ground pepper. Add more lemon if you like a more acidic sauce.

While the sauce is simmering, cut the duck into six pieces, including two legs with thighs and two breasts cut in half. You can freeze the wings and back for stock and for later use.

To serve, warm a nonstick pan on medium heat and add duck pieces skin side down. When skin is crispy, transfer to serving plates, strain gravy into a vessel, and pour sauce over the duck.

STUFFED PEPPERS

*S*tuffed bell peppers are one of the few recipes in Cipe's collection that bridge her Old World Jewish cuisine with what was (and still is) popular in American kitchens. These days, however, the green bell pepper is considered less flavorful and less glamorous than the warmer hues. This recipe calls for yellow, orange, or red, but green will make for a pleasing retro version. Quinoa and ground chicken offer a good vehicle for Cipe's sweet, ginger-inflected seasoning, hinting at Asian flavors. Be sure to cook the quinoa ahead of time, or start it before beginning the rest of the process so that it'll be done when it's time to fill the peppers.

108

6 bell peppers, halved and stem, seeds, and pith removed

1 tbsp chicken fat or oil

2 scallions, chopped finely, all white and some green part included

½ tsp minced fresh ginger

1 lb ground chicken (higher fat content of ground thighs is optimal)

½ cup cooked quinoa

1 tsp brown sugar

1 tsp soy sauce

In a shallow pan, heat chicken fat. Add scallions and ginger and stir gently for about 1 minute, not allowing too much browning. Add ground chicken and stir gently to brown meat lightly. When cooked through, turn off heat and mix in quinoa, sugar, and soy sauce. Taste and adjust salt level as desired.

Preheat oven to 400°. Spoon filling into pepper halves until evenly distributed. Place peppers into a medium-size baking dish with 2-inch sides, then place that dish into a larger dish filled with ½-inch of water to create steam. Cover the entire thing with foil and bake for 35–40 minutes, until peppers have softened. Remove foil and cook 5 more minutes to crisp the top of the filling.

LAMB STEW

This recipe nods toward the culinary trends of New York City in the 1940s.

Lamb was and still is a stylish meat, popular for entertaining, and the painting that accompanies Cipe's recipe, of the Super A&P Market, would have been a symbol of modern, urban, *American* living—one of the few paintings that depicts a place instead of a dish.

2 lbs lamb shoulder (stew meat), cut into ½-inch cubes, salted with 2 tsp kosher salt, 1 day in advance

2 tbsp olive oil

2 medium yellow onions, medium diced

1 bunch carrots or about 5 large, thinly sliced on a bias

10 whole cloves garlic, peeled

3 bay leaves

6 thyme sprigs, de-stemmed

freshly ground pepper

½ orange

½ cup white wine

2 cups vegetable, chicken, or lamb stock (plus more if needed)

1 cup green fresh chickpeas (alternatively you can use frozen green chickpeas or canned garbanzos)

yogurt or sour cream (for finishing)

One day ahead: season lamb with salt and refrigerate.

Warm the olive oil in a large Dutch oven over medium-high heat. When the oil is hot but not smoking, add the lamb cubes and sear for about 10 minutes, browning on all sides. Add onion, carrots, garlic, bay leaves, thyme, and pepper. Stir well. Cook on high heat for about 2–3 minutes or until fragrant. Add white wine and squeeze juice of halved orange into the pot, then drop in the skin. Add stock and lower heat to medium-low. Cover with a lid.

Simmer the stew for about 1 hour, stirring every 10 minutes. If needed, add more stock to the stew so it does not scorch on the bottom, but avoid creating too much liquid.

After 30 minutes, add chickpeas and cover and cook for another 30 minutes. The stew is done when lamb is tender and onions have broken down. Stew can be served immediately or saved and reheated. Serve with a generous dollop of yogurt or sour cream.

109

FISHKALACHA

There are two recipes for "kalacha" in Cipe's collection—one has the elements of a traditional meatloaf and is, in fact, called meatloaf, while the other is a meatball simmered in stock.

There is no fish in "fishkalacha," but the technique mimics one used for making "mock" gefilte fish—balls of vegetables and chicken simmered in stock. The results are quite tasty. In this update the meatballs contain breadcrumbs, which help maintain their form, and fresh herbs add a bit of complexity. The end result is essentially a dark, rich onion jam surrounding tender meatballs. Delicious on toast or, as Cipe suggests, with a baguette for ripping and dipping.

3 oz day-old bread, crusts removed

½ cup whole milk

4 onions

2 tbsp chicken fat or butter

1 tsp brown sugar

1 lb ground beef (85-percent lean)

2 tsp salt

3 grinds pepper (or to taste)

1½ cups chicken stock

1 tbsp fresh Italian parsley, minced

Tear bread pieces, then pulverize into crumbs in a food processor. Transfer to a small bowl and add the milk. Allow to soak while doing the next steps.

Slice 3 onions into rings. Heat chicken fat or butter in deep skillet and add onions and sugar, then cook until onions begin to soften. Add a small amount of stock or water to keep them well moistened and prevent sticking as they cook down, about 10 minutes.

Dice the fourth onion finely and add to a large bowl, then mix with the ground beef, salt, pepper, soaked breadcrumbs, and parsley. The mixture should be thick enough to form easily into balls without falling apart. If it's too wet, add more breadcrumbs a little at a time to reach desired thickness.

Add stock to the skillet with the onions. Bring to a simmer while forming the meat mixture into golf-ball size spheres using an ice cream scoop or spoon. Place meatballs into simmering onions, cover, and cook for 12 minutes, until done.

Serve on toast or with bread on the side.

KALACHA/MEATLOAF

*his is one of the first recipes
I tried from Cipe's book.*

Meatloaf: it seemed straightforward enough. The ingredients lined up with my idea of tradition—ground beef, tomatoes, onions, eggs, breadcrumbs, and seasoning. I followed her steps and ended up with . . . a delicious meat sauce. There was no loaf. The processing of the tomatoes on a grater yielded so much extra water that the dish couldn't take shape. It was soft, saucy. Delicious, but not what it claimed to be. Below is a lightly revised version that promises something more sliceable, and perhaps a bit fresher tasting with the use of a home-cooked tomato sauce for finishing. If you're in a hurry or it's not tomato season, using jarred sauce is an easy option.

FOR SAUCE

*6–7 medium ripe red
tomatoes (early girl, Roma,
or San Marzano)*
1 tsp kosher salt
2 tbsp extra virgin olive oil
2 tbsp water

FOR MEATLOAF

*1 lb ground beef (chuck or top
sirloin)*
1 large egg
½ cup breadcrumbs
1 green onion, thinly sliced
1 clove garlic, minced
*2 tbsp pistachios or pine
nuts, roughly chopped*
1 tbsp sage, finely chopped
1 tbsp parsley, finely chopped
1 tsp kosher salt
*½ tsp freshly ground black
pepper*

Preheat oven to 325°. Core and chop the tomatoes into bite-size pieces. Place a medium cast iron skillet over medium heat and add the tomatoes, then season with salt. Add olive oil and water and stir well, cooking until tomatoes break down, about 8–10 minutes. When done, transfer ⅓ of the sauce to a bowl and set aside.

In a large bowl combine the ground beef, egg, breadcrumbs, green onion, garlic, nuts, sage, parsley, salt, and pepper. Mix the ingredients with your hands until well combined, then shape the mixture into a smooth loaf and place it in the skillet (where ⅔ of the sauce should be waiting).

Cover the skillet and cook the meatloaf over medium-low heat for 20 minutes. Turn off the heat, pour the remaining tomato sauce over the meatloaf, and transfer to the oven. Bake for 20 minutes. When done, transfer the meatloaf to a cutting board, slice into ¾-inch slices and serve on a platter with tomato sauce.

112

SCHNITZEL

I t's hard to go wrong with breaded, fried meat.

This recipe is very easy, and can be made heavier or lighter depending on how you serve it. The traditional German schnitzel would often be served with pasta-like spaetzle, but a side of cabbage slaw or sautéed vegetables is a fresher alternative.

1 medium yellow onion, diced
2 cloves garlic
1 large egg
1½ lbs ground veal
2 tsp kosher salt
1 tsp freshly ground pepper
1 tsp ground caraway seed
5 oz French bread, crust trimmed off
3 tbsp vegetable or neutral oil (such as canola or peanut)

In a mortar or small food processor, grind the yellow onion and garlic into a smooth paste, working in batches if necessary, then place in a medium-size bowl and set aside. Tear the bread into small pieces and place them in a food processor, then pulse into small, relatively uniform crumbs. Transfer to small bowl and set aside.

In the bowl with the onion and garlic paste, add egg, veal, salt, freshly ground black pepper, caraway seed, and 2 tablespoons of your freshly made breadcrumbs. With a wooden spoon or your hands, mix well to combine all ingredients.

To assemble the schnitzel, measure out ¼ cup of the ground veal mixture, form it into a ½-inch-thick patty, then sprinkle generously all over with breadcrumbs. Place patty on a platter or baking sheet and continue these steps until all of the mixture has been formed.

To pan fry, pour oil in a small nonstick pan over medium-high heat. Working in batches, cook patties on each side for about 3–4 minutes or until golden brown. Transfer fried patties to a paper-lined plate to collect excess oil.

113

STUFFED SKIRT STEAK WITH CHARD, MUSHROOMS, AND BREADCRUMBS

Cipe's recipe for stuffed veal breast was one of the first I tried after finding her cookbook.

Locating veal was not as easy as I thought it would be, even at specialty butchers. So in adapting this for the modern cook, we decided to go with skirt steak, which can be found easily, is relatively inexpensive, and lends itself well to stuffing. The result is tasty and looks elegant, so it would be great for entertaining—something Cipe obviously knew!

2 tbsp olive oil

1 tbsp butter

1 shallot

8 oz white or cremini mushrooms, chopped

1 bunch rainbow or Swiss chard, chopped

8 oz breadcrumbs

2 tbsp fresh herbs (combination of thyme, rosemary, sage, oregano)

3 lbs skirt steak

cooking twine

Preheat oven to 375°.

Heat 1 tablespoon of oil and 1 tablespoon of butter in an oven-proof sauté pan. Add chopped shallot and cook 1–2 minutes, until soft. Add mushrooms and turn heat down slightly to allow mushrooms to cook without burning the shallot. Once the mushrooms release their water and begin to shrink, add chopped chard. Once chard has wilted, add breadcrumbs and herbs and season the mixture generously with salt.

Lay steak flat and spread filling across the top in an even layer. Carefully roll the steak from one end to the other, then tie securely with twine.

Wipe out the sauté pan and heat another tablespoon of oil. Sear the steak on all sides to get a crust. Transfer pan to the oven and roast until the meat is done but still a little pink on the inside. It's okay to slice into it to check, since it will be sliced for serving.

When done, slice and arrange on a platter.

CHICKEN FRICASSEE WITH MEATBALLS

I f you look up fricassee on the Internet today, plenty of recipes appear, but none of the most common or popular resemble what Cipe presents to us in her book.

Typical fricassee from, say, Martha Stewart, is a braise of chicken breasts or legs, while Cipe's is clearly a dish designed to use up parts of the chicken that were not already consumed in a roast or soup. This fricassee simmers gizzards and giblets with small beef meatballs, then thickens the whole thing with flour at the end. It was tough to think about how to approach an "update" to this that would not abandon the original intent, and when I asked Mimi Sheraton, grand dame of Old World Jewish cuisine, how she might go about it, she simply said: I wouldn't. So certain was she that this dish is perfect and oughtn't be modernized that we decided our update would simply be her version, which is well-tested and much beloved. This originally appeared in Mimi Sheraton's book, *From My Mother's Kitchen: Recipes and Reminiscences* (1979).

115

1 lb chicken giblets, to include gizzard and heart (but not liver), neck, backbone, and, if you like, chicken wings

½ lb ground lean chuck

1 small egg

½ clove garlic, crushed in a press, or 2 tsp grated onion

salt and black pepper

1 tbsp fine, dry breadcrumbs, as needed

2 tbsp schmaltz, margarine, or sweet butter

1 large onion, peeled and finely chopped

1½ tbsp sweet paprika or 1 tbsp paprika plus 1½ tsp hot paprika

1–2 cloves garlic, peeled and cut in half vertically

1 cup water, as needed

Clean the giblets, removing all skin and bits of fat. Gizzards should be scalded for 2–3 minutes in boiling water. Mix the chopped beef with the egg, crushed garlic or grated onion, 1 teaspoon salt, and ¼ teaspoon black pepper (or adjust to taste); add just enough breadcrumbs to make the mixture firm enough to mold into balls. Toss the ingredients lightly with a fork or the mixture will become too compacted and the meatballs will be hard. Shape into tiny meatballs, each about the size of a hazelnut.

Melt the fat in a 2-quart saucepan or casserole. Add the chopped onion and sauté very slowly until it is completely soft and bright yellow; do not let the onion brown. Stir in the paprika and sauté for a minute or two, or until it loses its raw smell. Add the cut-up garlic and 1 cup water.

Place the giblets and meatballs in the pan and add more water as needed to come about halfway up the meats. Add a little salt and pepper, half cover, and simmer gently but steadily for about 30 minutes, or until the giblets are tender and the meatballs are well done. Check frequently to see if more water is needed. Serve plain or with steamed white rice.

116

STUFFED CABBAGE

Cipe's recipe for stuffed cabbage seems very traditional until you get to the end, where she takes a surprising turn.

The classic dish of ground beef and cooked rice steamed in cabbage leaves gets doused, at the end, in a concoction of soaked gingersnaps, honey, and lemon juice. A sauce of soggy cookies! This was a surprise to me at first, and not a tempting one, but as I learned from Mimi Sheraton, this was a typical approach to adding flavor and depth, while also gaining a binding agent. Indeed, the cookie mixture created, in effect, a sweet and sour sauce, although not one I'd yearn for. In the update, we've eliminated the gingersnaps and instead called for fresh ginger mixed with lemon and honey to achieve the same effect. The result is tasty and a little more unusual than the plain tomato sauce called for in most stuffed cabbage recipes.

117

¼ cup basmati rice

1 large green cabbage (2½–3 lbs)

1¾ lbs lean ground beef

2 large yellow onions, divided, 1 diced small, 1 thinly sliced

1 bunch flat-leaf parsley, finely chopped

1 large egg

1 tbsp sugar

2 tsp kosher salt

1 tsp freshly ground pepper

1 28-oz can crushed tomatoes

2 tbsp honey

juice of 1 lemon

1 tsp freshly grated ginger

2 tsp salt

Preheat oven to 350°.

Rinse rice in a small strainer or bowl two or three times to remove excess starch. In a small pot, bring ½ cup of water to a boil then add the rice and reduce heat to low, season with salt, and simmer with a lid for about 5 minutes or until water is fully absorbed. Once the rice is done cooking, transfer the grains to a large mixing bowl to cool.

In a large pot, bring 4 quarts of salted water to a boil. While water is heating, core the center of the cabbage by inserting a sharp paring knife and cutting around the hard center. Use a fork to pull and release the core. When the water is boiling, drop in the cored cabbage, bottom side down, and cook with lid on for 10 minutes. When done, transfer to a rimmed baking sheet and let cool. Do not discard water; you may need to use it again if the inner leaves of the cabbage are not fully softened for rolling.

While the cabbage is cooling, make the filling. In the bowl where the rice grains have cooled, add ground beef, finely diced onion, finely chopped parsley, egg, sugar, kosher salt, and freshly ground pepper. Mix well with your hands. Once the cabbage has cooled, gently separate the leaves, being careful not to tear them. You should yield about 16–18 whole leaves. Take any torn or non-usable leaves and chop them roughly. Place the chopped leaves in a medium-size pot and add sliced onion, can of tomatoes, honey, lemon juice, grated ginger, and salt. Heat on medium, stir well, and cook until fragrant.

To make rolls, place a large spoonful of filling just below the center of a cabbage leaf. Starting at the rib end, roll over the filling, folding the sides in and tucking them into the roll as you reach the soft top of the leaf. Place the package on a baking sheet and continue filling the leaves until all are used.

Pour half of the tomato sauce into a 9-by-13-inch baking pan. Place the cabbage rolls tightly side-by-side on the tomato sauce, then cover with remaining sauce. Cover pan with aluminum foil and bake on the middle oven rack for 1½ hours.

118

POTTED LIVER AND ONIONS WITH A SOFT EGG

Chopped liver is such a classic Jewish "appetizing" food, and yet not everyone finds it truly appetizing.

Cipe followed the traditional approach of putting hard-cooked egg into the mix, along with well-cooked onions. The result has the familiar metallic tang of liver and the richness of all the fat and protein packed in. In this new version, the egg is separated from the liver and served soft-boiled, alongside a piece of toast. It would be as good for breakfast as for dinner.

2 eggs
2 tbsp unsalted butter
2 medium yellow onions, sliced lengthwise
3 sprigs thyme
¼ cup heavy cream
½ lb chicken livers, rinsed and pat dry
kosher salt
freshly ground black pepper

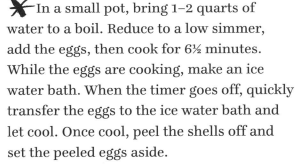

In a small pot, bring 1–2 quarts of water to a boil. Reduce to a low simmer, add the eggs, then cook for 6½ minutes. While the eggs are cooking, make an ice water bath. When the timer goes off, quickly transfer the eggs to the ice water bath and let cool. Once cool, peel the shells off and set the peeled eggs aside.

Heat a small Dutch oven or pot on medium-high heat and add the butter. Once the butter is melted, add the sliced yellow onions and the thyme sprigs and cook, stirring frequently, for about 4–5 minutes, until onions have softened and lightly browned. Add the heavy cream and stir to combine well.

Lower the heat to low-medium, add the chicken livers, and stir to combine. Cook for about 10 minutes or until chicken livers are just cooked through with a slight pink hue in the middle. Season with salt and freshly ground black pepper. Serve the liver and soft egg with a piece of buttered toast.

119

KASHA

With all the enthusiasm for whole grains these days, one would think that kasha, or buckwheat groats, might be having a resurgence.

But they are far less popular than farro, barley, quinoa, and steel-cut oats or oat groats. After trying Cipe's simple recipe for them, which calls for stirring an egg into the raw grains and toasting the mix before cooking (a preparation reminiscent of risotto), one can't help imagining applying her technique to some of our more trendy grains. The result is fluffy and a little rich and, as she says, you can eat them with a savory dinner or sweet breakfast.

1 cup buckwheat groats
1 egg
2 cups boiling water
1 tbsp butter
1 tsp salt

Put groats in a heavy saucepot. Crack the egg directly into the pot and stir, toasting the mixture over medium heat until the buckwheat smells fragrant (but careful not to burn!). Add the boiling water to the pot, reduce to simmer, stir in butter and salt, cover, and cook for 25 minutes.

WILD RICE

C ipe's illustration for cooking wild rice is one of the few from her book that shows up in various other places where her artistic hand left its mark.

She used it in several magazines and in a seasonal card, and one can see why—the shape and texture of the clay pot, the satisfying symmetry of the colander perforations, the fabulous detail on the porcelain teacup, which would have been used for measuring out the rice—it's all there. Though the image is one of the more ornate, the recipe is one of her simplest, just a formula for making a pot of rice, seasoned with sautéed onion and mushrooms at the end.

One note: in her original recipe, the notation seems to call for 2 quarts of water, which is 8 cups. That ratio is far off base for a single cup of uncooked rice, so we took it as an error and adjusted to 2 cups, not quarts.

**1 packet dried
  wild mushrooms
1 cup wild rice
2 cups water
½ tsp salt
1 tbsp butter
1 shallot**

Place dried mushrooms in a bowl with some warm water and allow to rehydrate while doing other steps. Once hydrated, chop into small pieces.

Rinse the rice until water runs clear. Add to saucepot and pour in water and salt. Cover, bring to a boil, then simmer for 25–30 minutes until water is absorbed and grains are fluffy. If using brown rice, the cooking time will be longer. Meanwhile, melt butter in a sauté pan, cook shallot until softened, then add chopped wild mushrooms and cook another 5 minutes. Season with salt and pepper. Combine with rice and serve.

121

BULBENICK
(Grated Potato Cake)

A t its heart, bulbenick is a baked dough of shredded potato—a bit like a giant Hanukkah latke minus the onion (and the frying).

In Cipe's sketchbook, the only painting that she reworked was the bulbenick, which has a flap of paper pasted in, on top of which is one version of the recipe, made with yeast and left to rise; and beneath which is another without yeast.

Although bulbenick isn't among the most familiar Jewish foods we find today, it's beloved by those who grew up with it. Susan Warsinger, a holocaust survivor, wrote for the United States Holocaust Memorial Museum's Memory Project about her family's bulbenick:

> I remember the preparing and baking lasted all day. Huge piles of potatoes had to be peeled and grated and placed into immense bowls. Eggs, yeast, oil, and flour would be mixed into this batch, which had to rest for some time before it was ready to be placed on the prepared oiled trays that were about four times the size of cookie trays that I use in my home now. When the mixture had risen, everyone helped pour it onto the trays because the thickness had to be just right. If I remember correctly, I think it was about one-half of an inch.

This updated recipe uses baking powder to give the dish some lift, and fresh herbs for some added dimension. When pouring the batter into the pan, heed Warsinger's suggestion about thickness. If the layer is too thick, it won't bake through; if it's too thin, it'll become very crisp and brown and lose the cakey interior texture.

6 large russet potatoes
1 tbsp plus 1 tsp kosher salt,
    divided
2 eggs
2 tbsp butter melted, cooled
    to room temperature

1 cup flour
2 tsp baking powder
¼ tsp freshly ground pepper
½ bunch thyme, roughly chopped
1 tsp rosemary, roughly chopped

Preheat oven to 375°.

Peel the russet potatoes and then grate into a medium bowl. Alternately, you can pulse in small batches in a food processor to shred the potatoes into small pearl-sized pieces. When the potatoes are processed, season with 1 tablespoon of kosher salt and mix well. Let sit for 10 minutes, then with your hands, squeeze off any excess liquid into a sink. Add the eggs and melted butter and mix well to combine.

In a separate large bowl, add the flour, baking powder, teaspoon of kosher salt, freshly ground pepper, and chopped thyme.

Slowly add the potato-egg-butter mixture into the flour mixture until well combined and the batter consistency is wet yet moldable.

Scrape the batter into a well-buttered 10-inch-square baking dish (for a thinner cake, divide into two pans). Place the dish into the oven and bake for 45 minutes, until cooked through and surface is golden brown.

123

VEGETABLE STOCK

I n almost all of Cipe's soup recipes, the core of the dish involves making a vegetable stock—boiling what she calls "soup greens," then removing

them and proceeding with whatever ingredients distinguish the soup, whether potatoes or pasta or dumplings. To make all of these recipes even quicker, and possibly more flavorful, the stock itself can be made from the recipe below and used in any of her vegetarian soups.

1 white or yellow onion
2 leeks
2 celery stalks
4 carrots
2 parsnips
Optional: 8–10 cremini mushrooms (these add a more savory, umami quality)

 Rinse any dirt from the vegetables and throw them, whole, into a large stock pot. Onions do not need to be peeled and leeks can be kept whole, with green portion attached. Cover with 4–5 quarts of cold water, bring to a boil, then lower to a simmer and cook for 1–2 hours. When done, cool and strain out the liquid. Store unsalted and season when using the stock in a recipe. Stock can be refrigerated for a couple of weeks, or frozen almost indefinitely.

124

CHICKEN STOCK

here are two ways to make this chicken stock.

The ingredients are identical to the vegetable stock recipe but for the addition of the chicken itself. The stock can be made by using bones leftover from roasting chicken or it can be made with a fresh, raw, whole chicken. If you choose the latter approach, you will also end up with lots of poached chicken meat, which can be great for adding into a soup or making another dish (chicken salad, enchiladas, or anythingelse that calls for moist, cooked chicken).

1 whole, raw, skin-on chicken or bones left from roasting (should add up to about as many bones as are in one bird)
1 white or yellow onion
2 leeks
2 celery stalks
4 carrots
2 parsnips
Optional: 8–10 cremini mushrooms (these add a more savory, umami quality)

 Rinse any dirt from the vegetables and throw them, whole, into a large stock pot. Onions do not need to be peeled and leeks can be kept whole, with green portion attached. If using chicken bones, add the bones. If using a whole, raw chicken, place it in the pot with the vegetables. Cover with 4–5 quarts of cold water to fully cover the ingredients, bring to a boil, then lower to a simmer and cook for 1–2 hours. When done, let cool then strain out the liquid. Store unsalted and season when using the stock in a recipe. Stock can be refrigerated for a couple of weeks, or frozen almost indefinitely.

125

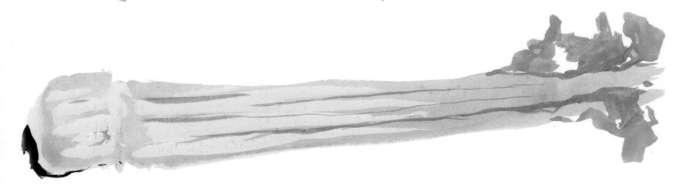

HAMANTASCHEN

The last seventeen paintings in Cipé's book were left unfinished, with the imagery in place but the recipe text missing.

For a few of them, the intended recipe remains a mystery, but others are obvious. She painted gefilte fish, for example, capturing its unmistakable nubby texture and the hot pink tint of beet-dyed horseradish in a jar on the side. And she painted hamantaschen, the triangular filled cookie prepared for Purim representing the tri-cornered hat of Haman, the defeated villain of the Purim story, and the triumph of good over evil.

Because Cipe left no recipe with this one, I turned to my mother, whose grandmother, Riva, would have been born around the same time as Cipe's mother, and who came from a similar region of Eastern Europe. My mom gave me Riva's recipe for hamantaschen—the one our family has used for generations. It yields a firm, not-too-sweet dough, so the filling is really the star. The prunes that dance across Cipe's page are the most traditional filling for hamantaschen, so that's what's included here, although poppy seed paste and various jams are also common. I even did a batch with chocolate hazelnut spread and was not disappointed in the least.

126

DOUGH

4½ cups flour (unbleached)
½ tsp salt
2½ tsp baking powder
1 cup sugar
3 extra large eggs, lightly beaten
½ cup whole milk
¾ cup butter, melted and cooled
1 tsp vanilla

FILLING

1½ cups pitted prunes
½ cup golden raisins
1 cup water
½ cup apple juice
Orange or lemon zest
2 tbsp milk
2 tbsp honey, heated

To make dough, mix all dry ingredients, then make a well in the center and add beaten eggs, milk, butter, and vanilla. Mix well, roll into a ball, wrap in plastic wrap, and chill for at least 3 hours.

To make filling, place prunes, raisins, water, and apple juice in a saucepan, bring to a boil, then simmer for 30–40 minutes until everything is soft and the liquid has mostly absorbed into the fruit. Be sure the liquid doesn't all boil off because the fruit will scorch. Add extra juice as needed while cooking to be sure fruit completely softens but does not burn. When pulpy and falling apart, remove from heat and stir in zest. This can then be pureed in a food processor for a smooth filling, or crushed with a fork or masher for a chunkier consistency.

Preheat oven to 375°.

To assemble cookies: Remove dough from refrigerator and cut into three chunks. On a floured surface, roll out each chunk to a ¼-inch thickness, doing in stages if there's not enough space. Using a 3-inch biscuit or cookie cutter, cut out circles. Next to your work area, set a small bowl with the 2 tablespoons of milk. Using a pastry brush, brush some milk around the outer edge of a circle of dough, then place a teaspoon of filling in the center, and pinch together the sides into a triangle shape. Repeat until all cookies are filled and shaped. Place on a cookie sheet lined with parchment and brush the cookies with warm honey. Bake for 10–12 minutes until golden.

127

ACKNOWLEDGMENTS

From the moment we found Cipe's sketchbook, this project has felt like it possessed its own minor magic, as if perhaps Cipe herself were nudging things along like a benevolent ghost. In so many instances, the right person appeared at just the right moment to lead us to the next stage of discovering Cipe's life and legacy. We are grateful to each person who's played a part in this process.

Thanks to our agent, Charlotte Sheedy, for her love of Cipe and her miraculous network; and to our wonderful editor, Nancy Miller, whose enthusiasm for this project was immediate and undying, and helped us trust in its potential. Thanks to Carol Burtin Fripp, Robert Fripp, Will Fripp, and Joel Corcos Levy for welcoming us into your homes and histories. Deep gratitude to Martha Scotford, whose rigorously researched book, *Cipe Pineles: A Life of Design* (1999), provided a foundation of knowledge from which to begin. Thanks to Christian Reynoso for his creativity and meticulous work in the recipe department; to the indispensable Celia Sack of Omnivore Books, and to the wonderful stewards of Cipe's archive at the Rochester Institute of Technology. Thanks to Steven Heller, Maira Kalman, Paula Scher, and Mimi Sheraton for their contributions to this book; to our book designers, Roberto and Fearn de Vicq de Cumptich, whose admiration for Cipe is evident throughout. Thanks to Caroline Paul for keeping the paintings safe from disaster; and Alexis Madrigal for knowing exactly who and what to ask. And to Trish Richman, Courtney Martin, Samin Nosrat, and many other friends who shared opinions, tested recipes, and otherwise showed their support.

RIGHT: *Photographer unknown. Reproduced in a newspaper,* Journal News, *September 11, 1985, accompanying article written by Nancy Cacioppo.*

INDEX

OF RECIPES

131

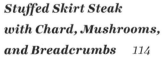
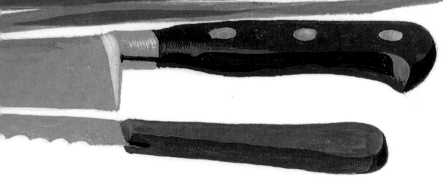

A NOTE ON THE AUTHORS

Cipe Pineles was the first female art director at Condé Nast, and the graphic designer and art director behind the popular magazines *Glamour*, *Seventeen*, *Charm*, and *Mademoiselle*. She was the first woman to become a member of the Art Directors Club, and in 1975 was inducted to the Art Directors Club Hall of Fame. She served as faculty and was later appointed director of publication design at Parsons School of Design. Pineles died in 1991 at age eighty-two and was posthumously awarded the 1996 AIGA Medal.

Sarah Rich is a writer, editor, and media strategist. She is co-founder of Longshot magazine and the Foodprint Project, co-author of the bestselling book *Worldchanging: A User's Guide for the 21st Century*, and former senior editor at *Dwell* magazine. She lives in Oakland, California.

Wendy MacNaughton is an illustrator and graphic journalist. Her books include *Meanwhile in San Francisco*, *Lost Cat*, *The Gutsy Girl*, *Knives & Ink*, and *Salt Fat Acid Heat*. She is a columnist for the *California Sunday Magazine* and co-founder of Women Who Draw, an organization that promotes and advocates for women illustrators.

Maria Popova is a reader and a writer, and writes about what she reads on Brain Pickings (brainpickings.org), which is included in the Library of Congress archive of culturally valuable materials. She has also written for the *New York Times*, *Wired UK*, and the *Atlantic*, among others, and is an MIT Fellow.

Debbie Millman is a designer, author, educator, and brand strategist. She is host of the award-winning podcast *Design Matters*, the world's first podcast on design; chair of the world's first Masters in Branding Program at the School of Visual Arts; the editorial and creative director of *Print* magazine; and President Emeritus of AIGA. She is the author of six books on design and branding.

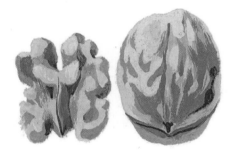